Aizu 11th generation
Izumi no Kami Kanesada

part 1

Noboru Toyama

© 2014 Noboru Toyama. All rights reserved.

ISBN 978-4-9907013-2-1

Toyama Publishing
Honcho 6-6-13
Sanjo, Niigata
955-0071 JAPAN

Translation: Marcus Sesko, Takao Fujimoto
Editor: Agata Maciak

TABLE OF CONTENTS

I. GREETINGS 5

II. ACKNOWLEDGEMENTS 7

III. THE CURRICULUM VITAE
   OF THE 11TH GENERATION KANESADA 9

IV. GENEALOGY OF THE AIZU SWORDSMITHS 10

V. GENEALOGY AND WORKMANSHIP OF THE FIRST TEN
   FURUKAWA KANESADA GENERATIONS 12

VI. WORKMANSHIP AND CHARACTERISTIC FEATURES
   OF THE 11TH GENERATION KANESADA 16

VII. THE CURRICULUM VITAE OF HIJIKATA TOSHIZŌ 19

VIII. CHRONOLOGICAL RECORD OF THE 11TH GENERATION
   KANESADA'S LIFE AND WORK 22

IX. PLATES OF THE 11TH GENERATION KANESADA'S WORKS 30

I. GREETINGS

First of all, the compilation of this catalogue on the 11th generation Kanesada would not have been possible without the assistance of Mr Toyama who is considered the leading collector of Kanesada´s works. Thus I would like to express my sincere gratitude to him. Also, I would like to express my gratitude towards the City of Aizu-Wakamatsu, the Aizu branch of the NBTHK, the Toshizō Hijikata Museum, and all those who provided us with precious swords and sword fittings from their collection in order to make this exhibition possible.

The 11th generation Kanesada came from Aizu, in Iwashiro province (present-day city of Aizu-Wakamatsu), and was active during the *Bakumatsu* and Meiji era. It is known that his swords were worn by local Aizu retainers and members of the Shinsengumi. An especially famous work of his became one of the favourite swords of the Shinsengumi vice-commander Hijikata Toshizō. Accordingly, the swordsmith Kanesada is not only known amongst sword collectors and regional historians, but also amongst those interested in the *Bakumatsu* era in general and the Shinsengumi in particular.

This catalogue presents an overview of Kanesada´s works from his earliest to his very last active period, so the reader will be able to become familiar with the changes in his signature and workmanship.

All proceeds from this catalogue go to the Fukushima Prefecture, the birthplace of Kanesada, which was hit so hard by the 2011 Tōhoku earthquake and tsunami. My thoughts and sympathies go out to the victims of this catastrophy and I hope that they can get over their loss and get back to normality as quickly as possible.

Kawashima Takatoshi (川島貴敏)

II. ACKNOWLEDGEMENTS

Special thanks:

Aizu Wakamatsu City
Nihon Bijutsu Token Hozon Kyokai
Hijikata Toshizo Shiryokan Museum

Iida Kyota
Ishizuka Takao
Kobayashi Hitoshi
Sakura Rikinori
Ikuno Masashi
Senoshita Akira
Tanobe Michihiro
Toyama Noboru
Nagasawa Kou
Hashimoto Yuuki
Hijikata Ai
Meada Nobuhiro
Myoga Yoshiya
Yagi Masayuki
Yoneyama Takahito
Yoneyama Ungai Takayori
Yoneyama Ungai Takamichi
Yoneyama Ungai Takatoku

Photos:

Hijikata Toshizo Shiryokan (Photo of Kusariboshi)
Hakodate Chuo library (Photo of Hijikata)
Yoneyama Takahito (Photo of 11th Kanesada, Hairyo-kosensho)
Photographs of the sword: Kawashima Kanako
Oshigata: Karita Naoharu (page no. 38)
  Fujishiro Tatsuya

Explanatory notes:

* "Aizu Tosho no Keifu (Genealogy)"
  and from "Shodai Aizu Kanesada (1st Kanesada)"
  till "Judai Aizu Kanesada (10th Kanesada)"
  is written in reference of "Aizu Token no bi"
  published by Aizu Wakamatsu City.
* Description of the swords are written by
  Noboru Toyama (Aizu Kanesada researcher)
  and Kawashima Takatoshi.

References:

* "Aizu Tosho Izumi no Kami Kanesada ni tsuite"
  by Yoneyama Ungai (Tokenbijutsu no. 52)
* "Aizu no Tosho" by Yoneyama Ungai (Aizu shidan)
* "Aizu Kanesada no Sakufu" by Toyama Noboru
  (Tokenbijutsu no. 571)
* "Tokyo Hohei kosho uchi no juichi dai Aizu
  Kanesada" by Iida Toshihisa (Tokenbijutsu
  no. 580)
* "Aizu Token no bi" by Kobayashi Hitoshi
  ("Aizu Wakamatsu shi 20-2")
* "Shin Rekishi gunso series ⑬ Hijikata Toshizō"
  by Gakken
* "Shison ga kataru Hijikata Toshizō" by Hijikata Ai
* "Nihonto Dai Hyakka Jiten" by Fukunaga Suiken
* "Keio nenkan Aizu Hanshi Jinmeiroku" by Aizu
  Goshi Shiryokan Kenkyujo

III. THE CURRICULUM VITAE OF THE 11ᵀᴴ GENERATION KANESADA

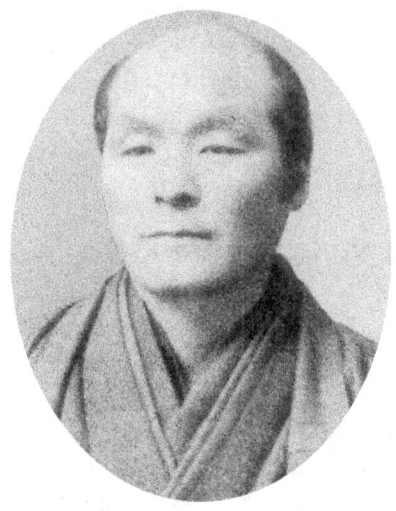

Furukawa Izumi no Kami Kanesada
(1837-1903)

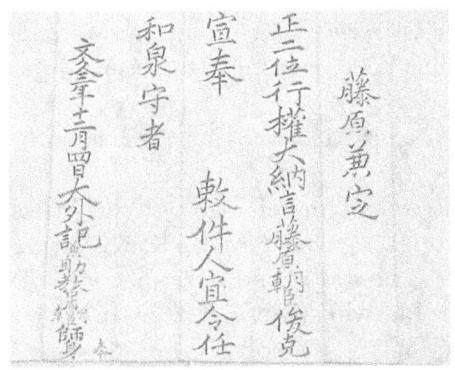

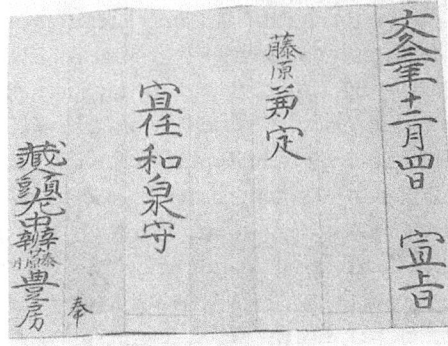

Official receipt of his honorary title
"Izumi no Kami"

The 11ᵗʰ Aizu Kanesada generation was born as son of the 10ᵗʰ generation Furukawa Ōmi no Kami Kanesada (古川近江守兼定) in Tenpō 8 (天保, 1837) in Aizu-Wakamatsu (会津若松). His youth name was "Tomoya" (友弥) which he changed to "Sei'emon" (清左衛門) when he was 29 years old. He was employed by the fief in Kaei 5 (嘉永, 1852) at the rather young age of 16 and made in his early years also *Daisaku-daimei* works for his father. He signed first with "Kanemoto" (兼元) but took the hereditary name "Kanesada" when he went in Bunkyū 3 (文久, 1863) to Kyōto to receive the honorary title "Izumi no Kami" (和泉守). (With that name change from Kanemoto to Kanesada, his father had changed his name to "Kaneuji" ([兼氏]).

Kanesada returned to Aizu in the first year of Keiō (慶応, 1865) when he was 29 years old but got on the fourth day of the fourth month of the very same year orders from the fief to move with all of his students to Echigo province. But as the fief had to strengthen its defensive measures, he was ordered back to Aizu just two months later. After that, Kanesada participated in the Boshin War and when Aizu-Wakamatsu Castle capitulated at the end of the ninth month Meiji 1 (明治, 1868), Kanesada had to leave the castle and was put under house arrest at Inawashiro (猪苗代) which is about 17 km to the northeast of Aizu-Wakamatsu.

In Meiji 2 (明治, 1870), Kanesada started, on request of the new government, to forge swords again, namely from the ninth month of that year for five years in the village of Kamo (加茂) in Echigo province. He returned to Wakamatsu in Meiji 7 (明治, 1874) to work for the newly founded prefecture of Fukushima. There are no dated blades known for 25 years from that time onwards. In the first month of Meiji 36 (明治, 1903) he was employed by the Army Artillery Weapons Factory (*Rikugun-hōhei-kōshō*, 陸軍砲兵工廠) which was based in Tōkyō and worked at the forge for Japanese swords erected there until his sudden death in the third month of the very same year. The 11ᵗʰ generation Kanesada lived to the age of 67.

IV. THE GENEALOGY OF THE AIZU SWORDSMITHS

The genealogy presented in this publication bases on the genealogies of the "Five Aizu Swordsmith Lineages and Six Families" (*Gokaji-rokke*, 五鍛冶六家) of Yoneyama Ungai's (米山雲外) *Aizu-tōshō-keifu* (会津刀匠系譜), put in order by Kobayashi Hitoshi (小林等). The "Five Aizu Swordsmith Lineages" comprises the most influential pre-Genroku (元禄, 1688-1704) lineages of swordsmiths working for the Aizu fief, and the "Six Families" are further six important lineages of swordsmiths which emerged in the late Edo period. The "Five Aizu Swordsmith Lineages" were:

1. Furukawa lineage (古川) (Kanesada)

This lineage goes back to the late Muromachi-period Seki swordsmith Kanesada who was employed by the Ashina family (蘆名), the *Shugo-daimyō* of Aizu, and moved to their lands, i.e. to Aizu. The lineage served, up to the Meiji era, successfully the subsequent rulers of these lands which were the Gamō (蒲生), the Uesugi (上杉), the Katō (加藤) and the Hoshina families (保科, later Matsudaira family [松平]). The Furukawa lineage is also referred to as Aizu Kanesada lineage and the 11th generation Izumi no Kami Kanesada was their last great master.

2. Shimosaka lineage (下坂) (Tameyasu)

The Aizu-Shimosaka lineage goes back to Tameyasu (為康) who worked for Katō Yoshiaki (加藤嘉明, 1563-1631) who was the *Daimyō* of the Matsuyama fief (松山藩, present-day city of Matsuyama in Ehime Prefecture) of Iyo province and followed his employer when the latter was transferred to Aizu in the fourth year of Kan'ei (寛永, 1627). The Aizu-Shimosaka lineage existed over ten generations until the early Meiji era and focussed on the production of *Yari* and *Naginata*. Most of their works do not feature an individual name and are just signed "Ōshū Aizu-jū Shimosaka" (奥州會津住下坂), but there are some later works from that lineage which do show an individual name in their *Mei*.

3. Miyoshi lineage (三善) (Nagamichi)

This lineage goes back to Nagakuni (長国) who came like Tameyasu to Aizu accompanying Katō Yoshiaki. The 3rd generation of the lineage and one of the best swordsmiths from Aizu was the famous Mutsu no Daijō Miyoshi Nagamichi (陸奥大掾三善長道). The lineage continued to exist over ten generations until the Meiji era.

4. Nakajō lineage (中条) (Michitoki)

The ancestor of this lineage was Nagatoshi (長俊) who was the second son of the aforementioned Nagakuni and thus the uncle of Miyoshi Nagamichi. The first smith who used the name "Michitoki" (道辰) and the greatest master of this lineage was the grandson of Nagatoshi. So he was the 3rd generation of this branch of the Miyoshi family and the 1st generation Michitoki. He founded around Genroku (元禄, 1688-1704) his own lineage, i.e. the Michitoki lineage, and signed with "Wakasa no Kami Fujiwara Michitoki" (若狭守藤原道辰). Incidentally, the characters for "Michitoki" usually read "Michitatsu" but this reading has a negative connotation as *"michi o tatsu"* means "the way ends", and so the reading "toki" was used for the second character (辰).

5. Suzuki lineage (鈴木) (Kanetomo)

The ancestor of this lineage was the 1st generation Tomonori (友則) who moved in Kan'ei 20 (寛永, 1643) to Aizu as he was hired by the then lord of the fief, Hoshina Masayuki (保科正之, 1611-1673), receiving a stipend for the support of five persons. The 2nd generation Tomonori was a student of Ōmi no Daijō Kanesada. He changed his name later to Kanetomo (兼友) and is thus counted as 1st generation Kanetomo.

The Edo period put an end to the successive wars which had begun in the late Muromachi period, and after the Shimabara Rebellion between the years 1637 and 1638, Japan was facing a steady peace. This and the stable government led around Genroku (元禄, 1688-1704) to a decreased demand for swords. Accordingly, also the output of the "Five Aizu Swordsmith Lineages" dropped noticeably between Genroku and Kyōhō (享保, 1716-1736) and the smiths were more like preserving the craft than supplying the demand for weapons. But things changed in the late Edo period when Japan faced pressure from outside and a distinctively growing instability from inside.

As a reaction, each fief started again to arm what in turn was beneficial to the craft of sword forging. The Aizu fief was of course no exception and besides the revival of the "Five Aizu Swordsmith Lineages", a new group of master smiths entered the stage whose six most representative lineages are summarized as the "Six Families". These are the schools of Sumi Motooki (角元興), Minagawa Munetoshi (皆川宗寿), Murata Kunimune (村田国宗), Wakabayashi Shigefusa (若林重房) Nagao Masataka (長尾将尊), and the Shimosaka branches (下坂別家). But there were of course also other individual swordsmiths working in Aizu at that time, like for example Kusakabe Shigemichi (日下部重道), which gave up sword forging and focused on the production of cutlery after the ban on swords had been issued in 1876. That means even though the turbulent *Bakumatsu* times meant a certain boom for the "Five Aizu Swordsmith Lineages" and "Six Families", they were connected to the feudal system and thus faced difficulties after the lost Boshin War and the abolition of the *Han* system and the return of all feudal lands to the emperor.

Anyway, from the beginning of the Edo period over the Boshin War and the ban on swords, the "Five Aizu Swordsmith Lineages" and "Six Families" gave rise to far more than one hundred swordsmiths. As indicated, certain smiths like Kusakabe Shigemichi or Wakabayashi Shigefusa changed their profession and worked after 1876 as manufacturers of carpenter or agricultural tools or provided clog shops (*Geta'ya*, 下駄屋) with carving tools. But because of the earlier so flourishing craft of sword forging in Aizu, the "Five Aizu Swordsmith Lineages", "Six Families" and their numerous students played an important role in the rise and spreading of the local cutlery production.

V. GENEALOGY AND WORKMANSHIP OF THE FIRST TEN FURUKAWA KANESADA GENERATIONS

1st generation

The 1st generation of Aizu's Furukawa lineage of Kanesada smiths was Furukawa Sei'emon Kanesada (古川清右衛門兼定). Sei'emon Kanesada was the son of the 3rd generation of Mino's Kanesada main line who in turn is also known as "Hiki-Sada" (疋定). There exists a legend on how this Furukawa Sei'emon Kanesada came to Aizu. According to this legend – of which several versions exist – the then ruler of the area, Ashina Moriuji (蘆名盛氏, 1521-1580), was in desperate need for swordsmiths and proclaimed that every swordsmith entering his lands had to be reported so that a possible employment could be negotiated. Sei'emon Kanesada was a religious man and so he went one day on a pilgrimage to see a famous Kokūzō statue (虚空蔵, Ākāśagarbha), the Bodhisattva of "boundless space treasure" and one of the eight great Bodhisattvas, located in the village of Yanaizu (柳津) in northern Mutsu province within the lands ruled by Ashina Moriuji. On the way back from Yanaizu, Kanesada decided to spend the night at a rather close hostel in Bange (坂下). The owner of the hostel followed his lord's orders and reported that a swordsmith was staying at his, whereupon Moriuji requested Kanesada to stay in Aizu to work for him. Kanesada saw this job offer as divine intervention of Kokūzō and named the sword ordered by Moriuji *"Rishō no goken"* (利生の護剣, about "Protection Sword by Divine Intervention"). Moriuji was very pleased with the finished work and so in the second year of Kōji (弘治, 1556) he granted Kanesada with lands in the village of Miyamae (宮前村) in the Yama district (耶麻郡) of the region (present-day Iwatsuki district [岩月] of Kitakata City [喜多方], Fukushima Prefecture) which yielded an annual income of 200 *koku* of rice. Incidentally, there exists a copper bell in the Shōfukuji Kannon-dō (勝福寺観音堂, *Jūyō-bunkazai*) just to the north of the former Miyamae which bears a signature of Kanesada.

The 1st generation Aizu Kanesada worked temporarily also for Date Masamune (伊達政宗, 1567-1636) in Sendai but his main place of occupation remained Aizu. In Tenshō 18 (天正, 1590), the Gamō family became the new castellans of Aizu's Kurokawa Castle (黒川城), replacing the old-established Ashina family. Kanesada received a salary of 200 *koku* from the Gamō and when Uesugi Kagekatsu (上杉景勝, 1556-1628) took over the lands between 1598 and 1601, he received a salary of 250 *koku* plus a stipend for the support of 20 persons. The 1st generation Aizu Kanesada died in the second year of Kan'ei (寛永, 1625). Extant works of him are rare.

Workmanship of the 1st generation Aizu Kanesada:

Sugata: *Shinogi-zukuri*, *Iori-mune*, thick *Kasane*, noticeable *Sakizori*
Jigane: standing-out *ō-Itame* mixed with *Mokume* and faint *Ji-nie*
Hamon: *Nioi-deki*, *Gunome* or *Suguha* mixed with *Nijūba* or *Togariba*
Bōshi: short *Komaru-kaeri*, *Midare-komi* or *Yaki-kuzure* which tends to *Kaen*
Nakago: *Higaki-yasurime* and *Kurijiri*, the *Mei* is applied with a fine chisel and the character for "Kane" (兼) looks like the character (魚)

2nd generation

The 2nd generation Aizu Kanesada's first name was "Magoichirō" (孫一郎) which he changed later to "Hisaya" (久弥). When Gamō Ujisato's (蒲生氏郷, 1556-1595) son Hideyuki (蒲生秀行, 1583-1612) moved from Utsunomiya (宇都宮) back to Aizu in 1601 taking over the lands from Uesugi Kagekatsu, he continued the 1st generation Kanesada's salary of 250 *koku* plus a stipend for the support of 20 persons. But besides of that, he ordered the 2nd generation Kanesada to change his smith name to "Tsunafusa" (綱房). After the death of Gamō Hideyuki's son Tadasato (蒲生忠郷, 1602-1627), Aizu was given to Katō Yoshiaki (加藤嘉明, 1563-1631). Yoshiaki took over Kanesada or Tsunafusa respectively for the same salary, i.e. 250 *koku* plus a stipend for the support of 20 persons.

The 2nd generation Aizu Kanesada made mostly *Katana* and *Wakizashi*. *Tantō* are not known, but there are some *Yari* extant.

Workmanship of the 2nd generation Aizu Kanesada:

Sugata: *Shinogi-zukuri*, *Iori-mune*, high *Shinogi*, deep *Sori*, as mentioned he made primarily *Katana* and *Wakizashi*, rarely he also made blades in more uncommon shapes like *Shōbu-zukuri* or *Kanmuri-otoshi*
Jigane: standing-out *Itame* mixed with *Mokume*, also with plentiful of *Ji-nie* or *Chikei*
Hamon: *ko-Nie-deki*, *Chōji-midare* mixed with *Gunome* or *Togariba*, also *Suguha* and *Nijūba*
Bōshi: long *Komaru-kaeri*, *Midare-komi* or *Yaki-kuzure* which tends to *Kaen*
Nakago: relative short, *Sujikai* or *Kiri-yasurime*, *Ha-agari Kengyō-jiri*, the *Mei* is applied with a fine chisel

3rd generation

The 3rd generation Aizu Kanesada's first name was "Mago'emon" (孫右衛門) which he changed later to "Magodayū" (孫大夫). His father worked as mentioned for Katō Yoshiaki but when the Katō were transferred to Iwami province in Kan'ei 20 (寛永, 1643), Mago'emon Kanesada stayed in Aizu and became a swordsmith of the subsequent Aizu ruler, Hoshina Masayuki (保科正之, 1611-1673), receiving a stipend for the support of five persons. The Hoshina were related to the family of the *Shōgun* and had therefore changed their name to "Matsudaira" at the end of the 17th century, and with the employment by Masayuki, the Furukawa Kanesada lineage served until the end of the Edo period continuously the Aizu-Matsudaira family. Anyway, in Keian four (慶安, 1651), Mago'emon Kanesada received by recommendation of the noble Hirohashi Dainagon family (広橋大納言) the honorary title "Ōmi no Daijō" (近江大掾). There are not many works extant of the 3rd generation Aizu Kanesada but most of them show an excellent *Deki*.

Workmanship of the 3rd generation Aizu Kanesada:

Sugata: *Shinogi-zukuri*, *Iori-mune*, wide *Mihaba*, thick *Kasane*, high *Shinogi*, deep *Sori*, he made mostly *Katana* and *Wakizashi* but rarely also some blades in more uncommon shapes like *Shōbu-zukuri*
Jigane: *Itame* mixed with *Mokume*, the *Hada* is tightly forged and the steel is bright, *Masame* appears in the *Shinogi-ji* and the *Hada* of some works tends to *Muji*
Hamon: *ko-Nie-deki*, *Chōji-midare* mostly mixed with *Gunome* and *Togariba*, also *Ashi* and *Sunagashi* can appear in the *Ha*
Bōshi: short *Komaru-kaeri* or *Yakikuzure*, rarely also *Bōshi* which almost appear as *Ichimai*
Nakago: relative short, *Sujikai-yasurime*, shallow *Kengyō-jiri* in *Kurijiri* manner, the *Mei* is applied with a thick chisel and he also signed with a *Naga-mei*

4th generation

The 4th generation Aizu Kanesada was hired in Kanbun 6 (寛文, 1666) for the same stipend to support five persons as the 3rd generation. Two years later in Kanbun 8 (1668), he received by recommendation of the noble Aburanokōji Dainagon (油小路大納言) the honorary title "Ōmi no Daijō" and took thereupon the first name "Ōmi" (近江). The third Aizu-Matsudaira lord Masakata (松平正容, 1669-1731) increased his stipend by three persons. The 4th generation Kanesada entered priesthood in Hōei 4 (宝永, 1707) and got thus later the nickname "Nyūdō Kanesada" (入道兼定).

Workmanship of the 4th generation Aizu Kanesada:

Sugata: *Shinogi-zukuri*, *Iori-mune*, high *Shinogi*, thick *Kasane*, noticeable taper, shallow *Sori*, i.e. his blades show a typical *Kanbun-shintō-Sugata*

Jigane: densely forged *Itame* mixed with *Mokume*, the *Shinogi-ji* shows *Masame*, some blades tend to *Muji* and some also show *Shirake*

Hamon: *ko-Nie-deki*, *Gunome* mixed with *Chōji*, also *Suguha*, *Ashi* and *Sunagashi* appear in the *Ha* and the most of his blades show a wide *Nioiguchi*

Bōshi: short *Komaru-kaeri*

Nakago: relative long, *Sujikai* or *ō-Sujikai-yasurime*, *Ha-agari Kengyō-jiri*, the *Mei* is applied with a thick chisel and he also signed in *Naga-mei*

5th generation

The 5th generation Aizu Kanesada's first name was "Kazu'emon" (数右衛門) which he changed later to "Ōmi". After his father's death, he succeeded at a young age as head of the family and had also to learn from his father's student, the 1st generation Suzuki Kanetomo (鈴木兼友). During his additional time as student of Kanetomo, his salary was shortened but upon his official employment by the fief in Shōtoku 3 (正徳, 1713), he received a stipend for the support of seven persons. The 5th generation Aizu Kanesada died in the 20th year of Kyōhō (享保, 1735) and no extant blades by him are known.

6th generation

The 6th generation Aizu Kanesada's first name was also "Kazu'emon" which he changed later to "Ōmi". He signed first with "Kanesada", but later changed his smiths name to "Kaneuji" (兼氏). He took over the family after his father's death in Kyōhō 20, receiving the same stipend for the support of seven persons. He died in Hōreki 2 (宝暦, 1752) and there are hardly any works known by him.

7th generation

The 7th generation Aizu Kanesada was the son of a certain Sakurai Michinao (桜井道直). He was adopted by the 6th generation and succeeded as head of the family in Hōreki 7 (1757), i.e. five years after his adoptive father's death. His first name was "Mago'emon" (孫右衛門) which he changed later to "Jidayū" (治太夫). It is said that he signed just with the *Niji-mei* "Kanesada" but there are no works known which could definitely attributed to him.

8th generation

The 8th generation Aizu Kanesada's first name was first "Dennai" (傳内) which he changed later to "Ōmi". He lived in the Ōmachi district (大町) of the castle town around Wakamatsu Castle and succeeded as head of the family in Tenmei 6 (天明, 1786) but his stipend was reduced by one to the support of now only six persons. Another change was that the Aizu Kanesada forge was now put under the control of the *Machi-bugyō* (町奉行), the local municipal administrator of the *Bakufu*. When he died in Bunka 12 (文化, 1815) at the age of 76, his son Yozō'emon (与惣右衛門) was too young to take over the family and so his student Kodama Takemori (児玉武守) was adopted into the family to act as transitional successor. There are no works known by the 8th generation Aizu Kanesada.

9th generation

The 9th generation Aizu Kanesada's first name was "Yozō'emon" (与惣右衛門). He signed first with "Kanesada" but changed his name later to "Kaneuji" (兼氏). After his father's death in Bunka 12 (1815), he was eventually rewarded for the service to the fief with the rank of Kōga (甲賀), a fief-interial *Samurai* rank which came along with the stipend for the support of six persons. But he was still employed as swordsmith and so he received a stipend for another person so that the family was again able to support seven persons. The 9th generation Aizu Kanesada died in Tenpō 4 (天保, 1833) at the age of 75. As mentioned, there are no blades extant which could definitely be attributed to one of the 5th to 8th generations Aizu Kanesada.

10th generation

The 10th generation Aizu Kanesada's first name was "Gyōzō" (業蔵) which he changed later to "Ōmi". First he signed with "Kanesada" but when the 11th generation received his honorary title "Izumi no Kami", he gave up this name and signed henceforth with "Kaneuji" (兼氏). It is said that he had also studied under the 4th generation Aizu Kanetomo (兼友) in his younger years. He was employed by the fief in Tenpō 6 (天保, 1835), i.e. two years after his father's death, receiving the rank of a Kōga and a stipend for the support of six persons. In Tenpō 12 (1841), his zeal and diligence in service earned him the *Samurai* rank of Kaisho-jiban (会所次番), and due to his continuous efforts, he was granted the rank of Dokurei (独礼) in Ansei 5 (安政, 1858). Not only the 11th but already the 10th generation Aizu Kanesada had trained a lot of students like for example Kaneharu (兼春), Kaneyoshi (兼吉) or Michinori (道則) and there are relatively many works of his extant.

Workmanship of the 10th generation Aizu Kanesada:

Sugata: *Shinogi-zukuri*, *Iori-mune*, thick *Kasane*, high *Shinogi*, shallow *Sori*, little tapering, altogether a grand and magnificent *Sugata*, he made mostly *Katana* and *Wakizashi* but there are also *Tantō* extant

Jigane: *Itame* mixed with *ko-Mokume*, sometimes also mixed with *Masame*, the steel is very tightly forged and bright

Hamon: *ko-Nie-deki*, *Suguha* or *ko-Gunome* mixed with *Chōji*, there are *Ashi* and *Sunagashi* and the *Nioiguchi* is mostly wide

Bōshi: long *Komaru* or *Ōmaru-kaeri*, occasionally also *Yaki-kuzure*

Nakago: the *Tang* is long and shows *Kiri* or *Katte-sagari Yasurime* and a *Ha-agari Kengyō-jiri*, the *Mei* is applied with a thick chisel and in a large manner

VI. WORKMANSHIP AND CHARACTERISTIC FEATURES OF THE 11ᵀᴴ GENERATION

Kanesada's blades might in sum best be described as overall well-balanced and most of them are outstanding when it comes to functionality and maybe also the conservative Aizu spirit of simplicity and strength plays a role here.

Sugata: All of his blades have a high *Shinogi* and so far I haven't seen one with a low *Shinogi*. This high *Shinogi* might be explained by his Yamato-influenced Mino roots but it is also possible that considerations on cutting ability led to the noticeably high *Shinogi*. At his time, i.e. in the *Shinshintō* era, wide and magnificent sword blades were greatly in fashion but Kanesada was also a master swordsman, so it is likely that his experience in handling a sword as a weapon resulted in his rather normally wide and not so exaggerated blades. This can also be grasped by attaching a handle to his blades, because doing so, the majority of them feels perfectly balanced. There are also oversized blades known made according to special orders but they too feels well-balanced when wielded. But the vast majority of his blades show a normal *Sugata*.

Jigane: Kanesada's *Jigane* can roughly be divided into a *Masame*-based forging, a dense *ko-Itame*, and an *ō-Itame* mixed with *ō-Mokume* and *Masame* and a tendency to *Nagare*. The steel has the blackish appearance which is typical for sword blades from the Tōhoku and Hokuriku region but it also has certain clarity and it shows *Ji-nie*. We know from some signatures that he used "old steel" (*Kotetsu*, 古鉄) or "old *Kotō* steel" (*Kotō no tetsu*, 古刀の鉄) and some of the blades made that way really look a bit like old *Kotō* swords.

Hamon: During the time he signed with "Kanemoto", he actually also tempered often a *Sanbonsugi*-based *Hamon* (for which the famous *Kotō*-era Kanemoto smiths were famous). Apart from that, he often tempered a *Suguha*, a wild and very *Nie*-loaden *Sōshū*-inspired *Hitatsura*, or a varied and lively *Hamon* modelled on old Shizu works (志津), and this great variety testifies to his great skill. *Tantō* in turn are mostly tempered in *Suguha*.

Bōshi: *Komaru-kaeri*, *Midare-komi*, also *Jizō*-like interpretations and *Hakikake* which make the *Bōshi* tend to *Kaen*.

Nakago: Due to the emphasis on actual use, his tangs are rather long but taper towards the tip. The *Yasurime* are *Sujikai* and the tip is a *Ha-agari Kengyō-jiri*. He signed with a thick chisel and in a powerful manner and he executed the character for "*Sada*" (定) with the lower radical (之) instead of (疋) just as the famous No-Sada did. Incidentally, this lower radical (之) reads "*No*", and this way of signing was what earned No-Sada his nickname. However, blades made in Kamo in Echigo province are mostly signed with a rather fine chisel and in a not so forceful manner. Or in other words, I haven't seen any Kamo blades signed with a thick chisel and in a powerful manner but further studies are necessary in this respect. When looking at the blades introduced later in this publication, we learn that almost a third of them bears inscriptions of the results of cutting tests performed by Kanesada himself. This demonstrates very well the great importance he attached to the usability and cutting ability of his blades. There are also some blades in this publication which were initially only signed on the *Omote* side and where the result of a cuttings test performed by Kanesada was added later to the *Ura* side. Also interesting to note is that results of cutting tests are no longer found after the beginning of the Meiji era.

Places of production: Kanesada worked mostly in four places, namely Aizu, Kyōto, Echigo and Tōkyō. The vast majority of the extant blades were made in Aizu and Echigo (e.g. in Kamo [加茂], Shibata [新発田] or Kannonji [観音寺]). Works from his short stay in Kyōto and from his last years in Tōkyō are rare.

The contrast of the photos was manipulated in order to show the texture of *Jitetsu* better.

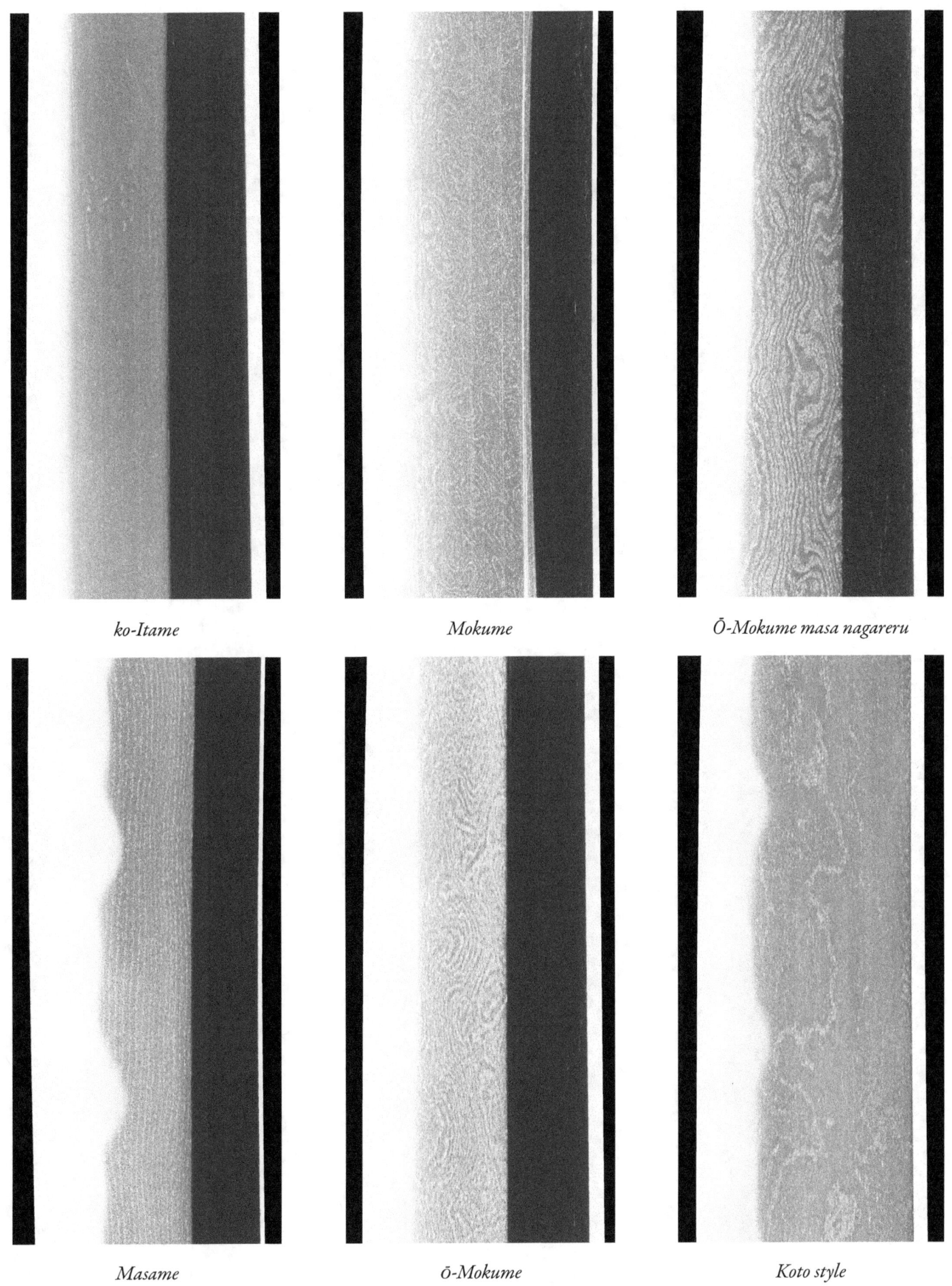

VII. THE CURRICULUM VITAE OF HIJIKATA TOSHIZŌ
(1835-1869)

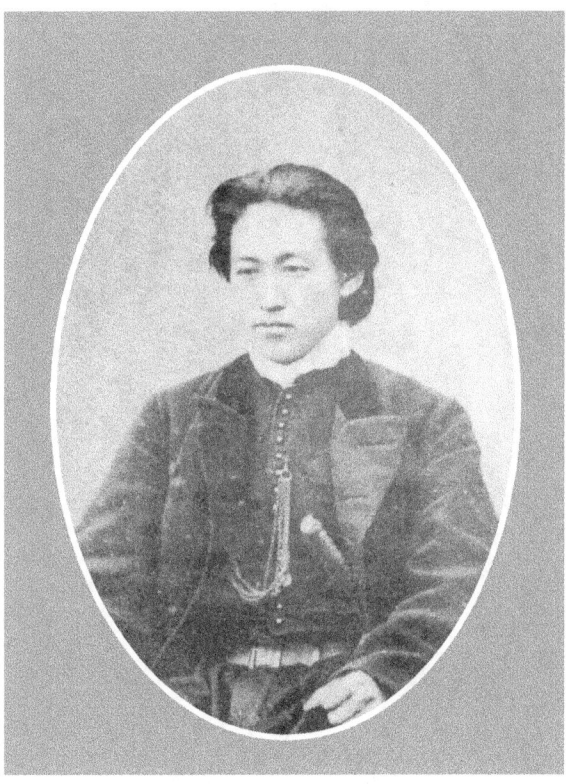

The Shinsengumi vice-commander Hijikata Toshizō (土方歳三) was born in the sixth year of Tenpō (天保, 1835) in the village of Ishida (石田村) in the Tama district of Musashi province (present-day Hino, a suburb of Tōkyō). The Hijikata were a well-to-do family of farmers but Toshizō was of a strong character already at an early age and always had the desire to become a *Bushi*. Hijikata spent his youth selling his family's *Ishida Sanyaku* (石田散薬, medicine for treating injuries such as bruises and broken bones) while practicing his self-taught *Kenjutsu* in duels with men from other schools of swordsmanship at different places. His brother-in-law, Satō Hikogorō (佐藤彦五郎), managed a Tennen Rishin-ryū dōjō (天然理心流), a school of swordsmanship founded around 1789 which later became to be known as the style practiced by several core members of the Shinsengumi.

Through Satō, Toshizō met Kondō Isami (近藤勇, 1834-1868), the later commander of the Shinsengumi, and was formally enrolled at the *Tennen Rishin-ryū* in Ansei 6 (安政, 1859). Due to his progress, Toshizō became eventually the vice master of the *Dōjō*. In Bukyū 3 (文久, 1863), the 14th Tokugawa-*Shōgun* Ieshige (徳川家茂, 1846-1866) was preparing to embark on a trip to Kyōto to meet the emperor, but loyalists to the emperor were already committing acts of murder and violence in the old imperial court. Responding to this trend, the Tokugawa Shogunate formed the protective Rōshingumi (浪士組), a group of 234 masterless *Samurai*, Hijikata Toshizō being one of them. In Kyōto however, the Rōshingumi split and thirteen members formed a group called Miburō (壬生浪, lit. "*Rōnin* of Mibu", Mibu being the then-suburb of central Kyōto where they were stationed) which was later renamed to Shinsengumi (新選組, lit. "Newly Selected Corps"). At the beginning, the group was composed of three major factions, Kondō Isami leading one of them, but one of the leaders was assassinated quite early, leaving just to factions. The two-part Shinsengumi submitted a letter to the Aizu fief requesting permission to police Kyōto and to counteract the revolutionaries who supported the emperor against the Tokugawa Shogunate. Their request was granted. Matsudaira Katamori (松平容保, 1836-1893), the then *Daimyo* of the Aizu fief, was namely responsible for policing Kyōto at that time.

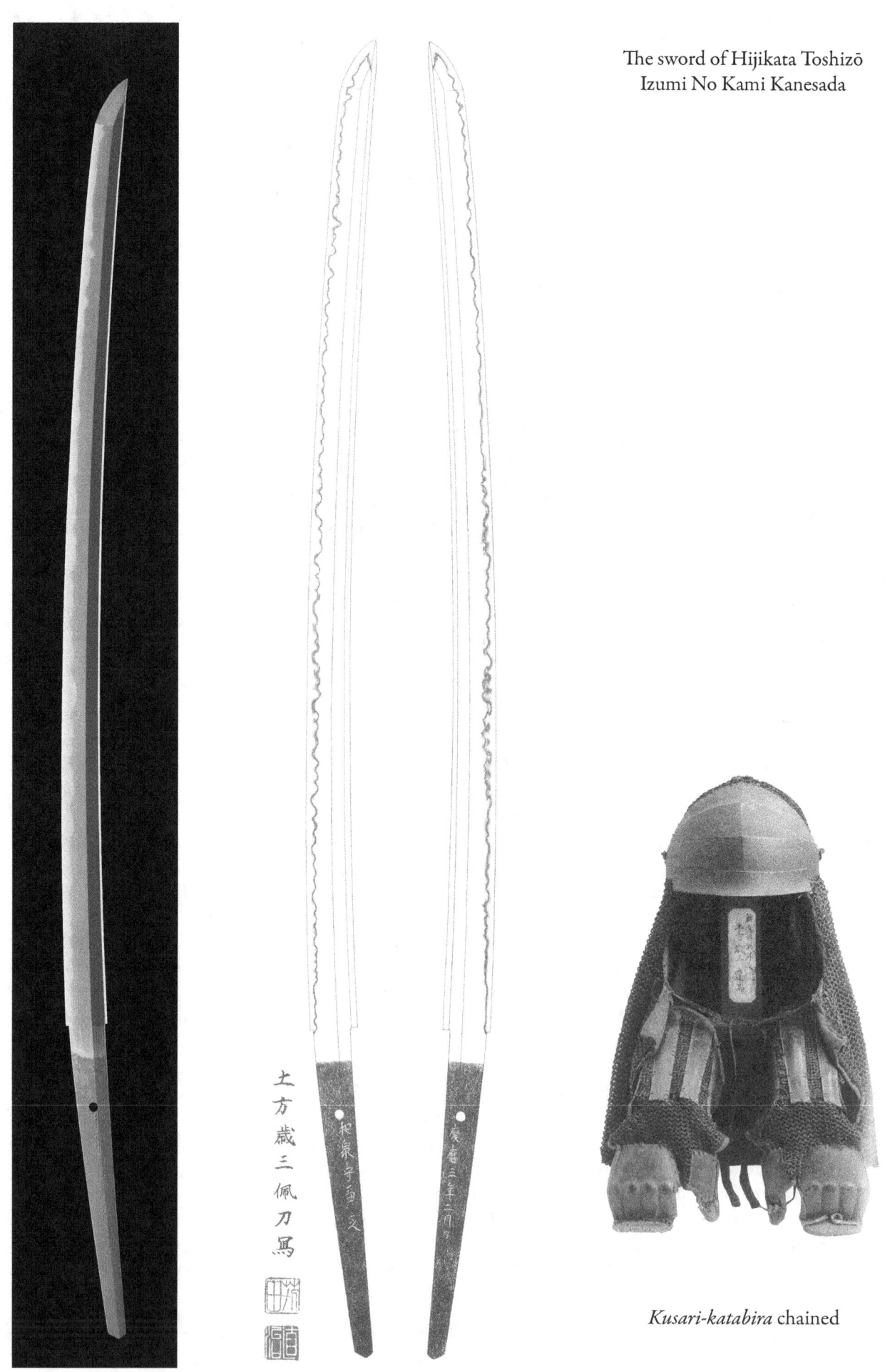

The sword of Hijikata Toshizō
Izumi No Kami Kanesada

Kusari-katabira chained

So Kondō and Hijikata attacked in 1864 the Ikeda Inn (Ikedya, 池田屋) in Kyōto which was the base for some anti-Tokugawa *Rōnin*. This incident went down in history as Ikedaya Incident and made the Shinsengumi famous overnight and this was also the time when Kondō became their sole leader, making Hijikata Toshizō and Yamanami Keisuke (山南敬助, 1833-1865) his vice-commanders. The regulations set up by the Shinsengumi within Kyōto were strict and Hijikata was known to be harsh in enforcing them, hence his nickname: "The Demon of the Shinsengumi". The Shinsengumi remained loyal to the Tokugawa-*Bakufu* and left Kyōto peacefully shortly after the withdrawal of Tokugawa Yoshinobu (德川慶喜, 1837-1913) in 1867. However, as they had been posted as security forces in Fushimi, they soon took part in the Battle of Toba-Fushimi (鳥羽・伏見の戦い) which broke out early in 1868 between pro-Imperial and Tokugawa *Bakufu* troops. As the *Bakufu* troops were defeated, Hijikata and his men left Kyōto and withdrew to Edo but participated in successive fightings like the Battle of Kōshū-Katsunuma (甲州勝沼の戦い) in Kai province and Nagareyama (流山) in Shimōsa province. Kondō eventually surrendered and was beheaded on the 25th day of the fourth month Meiji 1 (明治, 1868) at Itabashi (板橋) in Edo. After Kondō's death, Hijikata Toshizō led the Shinsengumi in their final battles against the new government, namely in Utsunomiya (宇都宮) in Shimotsuke province, in Aizu, and in Hakodate (函館) to defend the fortress of Goryōkaku (五稜郭) against the imperial troops. Goryōkaku was the main fortress of the short-lived Republic of Ezo (蝦夷) established by former Tokugawa retainers in what is now known as Hokkaidō. Imperial troops continued to attack by land and sea. In the final conflict of the revolution, on June 20 (lunar calendar: 5th month, 11th day), 1869, Hijikata was killed at the age of 35 while in combat on horseback by a bullet that shattered his lower back. His death poem reads: *"Yoshiyami wa Ezo ga shimabe ni kuchiru tomo tamashii wa azuma no kimi ya mamoramu."* (よしや身は蝦夷が島辺に朽るとも魂は東の君やまもらむ) – "Though my body may decay on the island of Ezo, my spirit guards my lord in the east."

VIII. CHRONOLOGICAL RECORD OF THE 11ᵀᴴ GENERATION KANESADA'S LIFE AND WORK

Year:	Age:	Stage in his life:	Signatures on extant works:	Important events:
Tenpō 8 天保, 1837	1	Born in Aizu as the son of the 10th generation Aizu Kanesada.		Rebellion of Ōshio Heihachirō (大塩平八郎).
Kaei 6 嘉永, 1853	16	Entered on behalf of the fief an apprenticeship as repair man of tools and implements	*Wakizashi:* "*Aizu-jū Kanemoto – Jūyūroku-sai saku*" (會津住兼元・十有六才作, "made by Kanesada from Aizu at the age of 16")	The Black Ships of Commodore Perry arrived at Uraga Harbor.
Kaei 7 嘉永, 1854	17	Made *Daisaku-daimei* works for the 10th generation Aizu Kanesada from this time onwards.	*Katana:* "*Ōshū Aizu-jū Fujiwara Kanesada – Kaei shichinen kinoe-tora kugatsu hi*" (奥刕會津住藤原兼定・嘉永七年甲寅九月日, "a day in the ninth month Kaei 7, year of the tiger")	Convention of Kanagawa concluded between Commodore Perry and the Tokugawa Shogunate.
Ansei 4 安政, 1857	20		*Katana:* "*Aihan-shin Kanesada Kanemoto chūseisshin shikamo sanmai-sei o motte kore o tsukuru – Ansei yon hinoto-hebi-doshi hachigatsu kichijitsu*" (會藩臣兼定兼元・抽精神以三枚製而造之・安政四丁巳年八月吉日, "made with special diligence and in the *Sanmai* technique by the Aizu fief retainers Kanesada and Kanemoto on a lucky day of the eighth month Ansei 4")	
Ansei 7 = Man'en 1 萬延, 1860	23		*Katana:* "*Mutsu Aiyō-shin Fujiwara Kanemoto chūseiryoku kore o tsukuru – Ansei shichi kanoe-sarudoshi nigatsu kichijitsu*" (陸奥會陽臣藤原兼元抽精力造之・安政七庚申年二月吉日, "made with special effort by the Aizu fief retainer Kanemoto on a lucky day of the second month Ansei 7, year of the monkey") *Wakizashi:* "*Aiyō-shin Kanemoto – Man'en gan sarudoshi shigatsu hi*" (會陽臣兼元・萬延元申年四月日, "a day of the fourth month Man'en 1, year of the monkey")	Sakuradamon Incident. The era changed from Ansei to Man'en in the third month of that year.
Man'en 2 = Bunkyū 1 文久, 1861	24	Killed a disrespectful disciple and withdrew but was pardoned and allowed to continue his craft.	*Tantō:* "*Aiyō-shin Kanemoto kore o tsukuru – Bunkyū gan kanoto-toridoshi hachigatsu kichijitsu – Kimibanzai*" (會陽臣兼元造之・文久元辛酉年八月吉日・君萬歳, "on a lucky day of the eighth month Bunkyū 1, year of the rooster – Long Life for the Sovereign")	American Civil War broke out. The era changed from Man'en to Bunkyū in the second month of that year.

Year:	Age:	Stage in his life:	Signatures on extant works:	Important events:
Bunkyū 3 文久, 1863	26	Was ordered to Kyōto and received there in the twelfth month of that year the honorary title "Izumi no Kami". Changed thereupon his name from Kanemoto to Kanesada.		Shimonoseki Campaign fought to control Shimonoseki Straits by joint naval forces from Great Britain, France, the Netherlands and the US against the Japanese feudal domain of Chōshū. Anglo-Satsuma War between the Royal Navy and Satsuma.
Bunkyū 4 = Genji 1 元治, 1864	27	Supported the imperial guards when the Hamaguri Gate Rebellion took place.		Ikedaya Incident which made the Shinsengumi famous. The era changed from Bunkyū to Genji in the second month of that year.
Genji 2 = Keiō Gannen 慶應, 1865	28	Returned from Kyōto to Aizu.	*Katana*: "Izumi no Kami Fujiwara Ason Kanesada – Keiō gan ushidoshi hachigatsu hi" (和泉守藤原朝臣兼定・慶應元丑年八月日, "a day of August, Keiō Gan-nen, year of the ox")	The era changed from Genji to Keiō in the fourth month of that year.
Keiō 2 慶應, 1866	29		*Katana*: "Izumi no Kami Fujiwara Ason Kanesada – Keiō ni toradoshi hachigatsu hi" (和泉守藤原朝臣兼定・慶應二寅年八月日, "a day of the eighth month Keiō 2, year of the tiger")	The Satsuma-Chōshū Alliance was formed to combine their efforts to overthrow the Tokugawa Shogunate.
Keiō 3 慶應, 1866	30		*Katana*: "Izumi no Kami Kanesada – Keiō sannen nigatsu hi" (和泉守兼定・慶應三年二月日, "a day of the second month Keiō 3") *Katana*: "Mutsu-shi Izumi no Kami Fujiwara Ason Kanesada – Keiō san – Kishima Jūhei no tame chūtanrensei" (陸奥士和泉守藤原朝臣兼定・慶應三・為木嶋重平抽鍛錬精, "Forged with special effort in Keiō 3 by the Mutsu retainer Izumi no Kami Fujiwara Ason Kanesada for Kishima Jūhei") *Katana*: "Aihan-shi Izumi no Kami Fujiwara Ason Kanesada – Keiō san hinoto-usagidoshi hachigatsu hi" (會藩士和泉守藤原朝臣兼定・慶應三丁卯年八月日, "a day of the eighth month Keiō 3, year of the hare")	*Taiseihokan*- restoration of the imperial rule.

Year:	Age:	Stage in his life:	Signatures on extant works:	Important events:
Keiō 4 = Meiji 1 明治, 1868	31	In the fourth month, he was ordered to work in the village of Kannonji in Echigo province but was ordered back to Aizu in the sixth month when the Battle of Hokuetsu occurred. In the eighth month, he succeeded as 11th generation Aizu-Kansada. Aizu-Wakamatsu Castle surrendered in the ninth month.	*Katana:* "Izumi no Kami Fujiwara Ason Kanesada – Keiō yon tsuchinoe-tatsudoshi nigatsu hi" (和泉守藤原朝臣兼定・慶應四戊辰年二月日, "a day of the second month Keiō 4, year of the dragon") *Tantō:* "Aizu-shi Izumi no Kami Kanesada" (會津士和泉守兼定・慶應四年八月日, "a day of August, Keiō 4") *Wakizashi:* "Dai Nihon kaji-sōshō Izumi no Kami Fujiwara Kanesada – Keiō yon tsuchinoe-tatsudoshi chūshū no hi" (大日本鍛治宗匠和泉守藤原兼定・慶應四戊辰年仲秋日, "Izumi no Kami Fujiwara Kanesada, master swordsmith of Japan, in the middle of August, Keiō 4")	Battle of Hokuetsu. The era changed from Keiō to Meiji on the ninth month of that year.
Meiji 2 明治, 1869	32	The 10th generation Aizu Kanesada passed away. The fief ordered him to Kamo in Echigo province.	*Katana:* "Iwashiro no Kuni-jū Izumi no Kami Kanesada – Meiji ni hebidoshi hachigatsu hi" (岩代国住和泉守兼定・明治二巳年八月日, "a day of the eighth month Meiji 2, year of the snake") *Tantō:* "Izumi no Kami Kanesada – Meiji ninen hachigasu hi" (岩代国住和泉守兼定・明治二年八月日)	The Boshin War ended.
Meiji 3 明治, 1870	33		*Katana: Iwashiro no Kuni-jū Kanesada – Meiji sannen nigatsu hi* (岩代國住兼定・明治三年二月日, "a day of the second month Meiji 3")	Common people were allowed to use surnames.
Meiji 4 明治, 1871	34	The 10th generation Aizu Kanesada passed away. The fief ordered him to Kamo in Echigo province.	*Katana:* "Iwashiro no Kuni-jū Izumi no Kami Kanesada – Meiji ni hebidoshi hachigatsu hi" (岩代国住和泉守兼定・明治二巳年八月日, "a day of the eighth month Meiji 2, year of the snake") *Tantō:* "Izumi no Kami Kanesada – Meiji ninen hachigasu hi" (岩代国住和泉守兼定・明治二年八月日) Homage to the Tathāgata Buddha of Inconceivable Light") *Tantō:* "Kamo ni oite – Izumi no Kami Kanesada – Meiji yon kanoto-hitsuji-doshi hachigatsu hi" (於加茂・和泉守兼定・明治四辛未年八月日, "a day of August, Meiji 4")	Abolition of the *Han* system.

Year:	Age:	Stage in his life:	Signatures on extant works:	Important events:
Meiji 6 明治, 1873	36		*Wakizashi:* "Izumi no Kami Kanesada – Meiji rokunen hachigatsu hi" (和泉守兼定・明治六年八月日, "a day of the eighth month Meiji 6")	Conscription order and land tax reform.
Meiji 7 明治, 1874	37		*Tantō:* "Dai Nihon Kamo Kanesada – Kigen nisengohyakusanjūyonnen nigatsu" (大日本加茂兼定・紀元二千五百三十四年二月, "second month of the 2,534th anniversary of the imperial era")	Saga Rebellion.
Meiji 9 明治, 1876	39	Returned from Kamo to Aizu and started to work for the Prefecture of Fukushima.		Haitōrei ban on wearing swords.
Meiji 25 明治, 1892	54	Presented *Katana* to the crown prince (the later emperor Taishō)	*Katana:* "Dai Nihon Kanesada – Kigen nisengohyakugojūninen nigatsu hi" (大日本兼定・紀元二千五百五十二年二月日, "a day of the second month of the 2,552nd anniversary of the imperial era")	
Meiji 28 明治, 1895	59		*Katana:* "Izumi no Kami Kanesada – Meiji nijūhachinen sangatsu jūkyūnichi" (和泉守兼定・明治二十八年二月十九日, "19th day of the second month Meiji 28")	The Treaty of Shimonoseki.
Meiji 35 明治, 1902	66		*Tantō:* "Kanesada – Meiji sanjūgonen ichigatsu futsuka" (兼定・明治三十五年一月二日, "second day of the first month Meiji 35")	First Anglo-Japanese Alliance.

Kodōgu (fitting)
Tsuba

Mei:
Omote: Hokuetsu Kamo-jū Izumi no Kami Kanesada
　　　　北越加茂住和泉守兼定
Ura:　*Meiji rokunen nigatsu hi*
　　　　明治六年二月日
　　　　A day of the second month Meiji 6 [1873]

Fuchigashira

Mei:　*Kanesada*
　　　　兼定

Here we have one of the extremely rare fittings of the 11th generation Aizu Kanesada, namely an en suite set of *Tsuba* and *Fuchigashira*. The *Tsuba* is large, of iron, in *Mokkō-gata* and *Nakabiku*. The surface is etched and mercury gilded, that means gold powder is mixed with mercury to form an amalgam which leaves only the gold on the surface after the mercury vaporizes when heated. This technique is usually applied to *Habaki* to create the so-called *Koke-habaki* (lit. 'moss habaki'). A *Koke* effect on *Tsuba* is usually achieved by the Tokin technique where mercury serves as a carrier for a gold foil. So we are facing quite an elaborate interpretation for a *Tōshō-tsuba*. The signature and date differ from signatures found on sword blades but this is because a different chisel was used. Apart from that, the *Mei* shows all the characteristics of Kanesada's signature and the condition of the set is excellent.

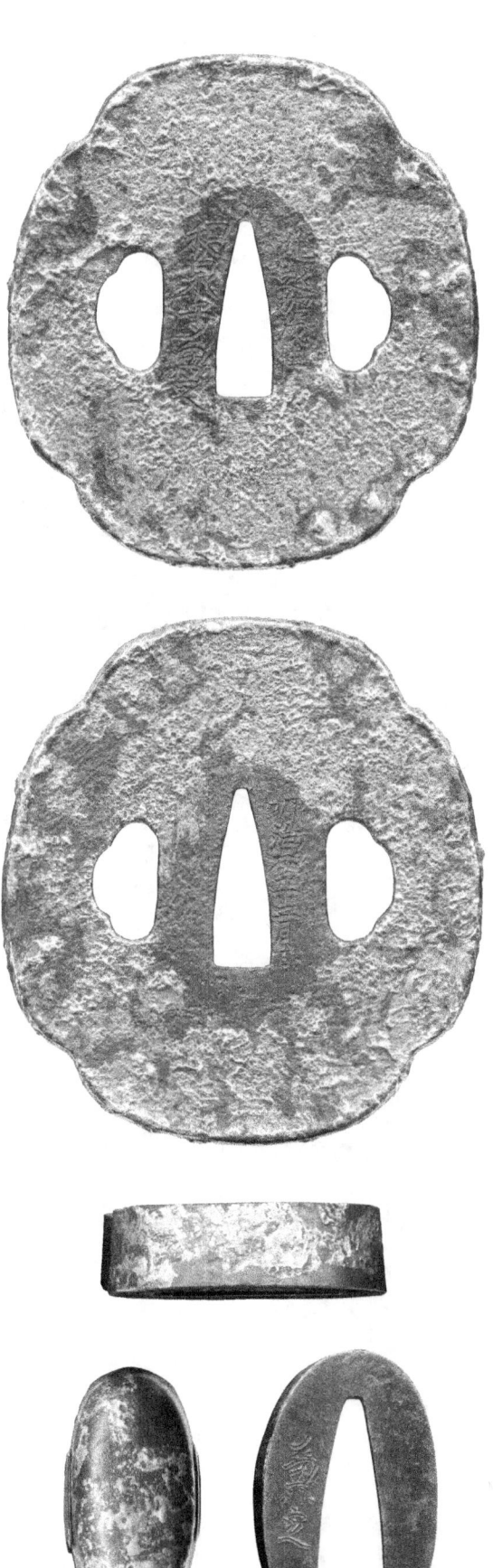

Aizu 11th generation Izumi no Kami Kanesada

會津十一代

和泉守兼定

IX. PLATES OF THE 11ᵀᴴ GENERATION KANESADA'S WORKS

Wakizashi

Mei:
Omote: *Aizu-jū Kanemoto – Jūyūroku-sai saku*
會津住兼元　十有六才作
Made by Kanemoto from
Aizu at the age of 16
Ura: *Ansei shichi sarudoshi nigatsu jūsannichi –
Egami Tokurin hosogoshi dotanbarai*
安政七申年二月十三日　江上徳郷細腰土壇拂
13ᵗʰ day of the second month Ansei 7
[1860], year of the monkey – Egami Tokurin
tested this blade on the consecrated testing
ground on a body with a slender hipbone
Nagasa: 1 *shaku* 3 *sun* 8 *bu* (41,8 cm)
Sori: 2 *bu* 5 *ri* (0,7 cm)

This blade looks at a glance just like an ordinary *Hira-zukuri Wakizashi* but we are facing here an important reference, namely what is thought to be the very first blade (extant) Kanesada made all by himself. The signature mentions "made at the age of 16" (*Jūyūroku-sai saku*, 十有六才作), but in an uncommon syntax which reminds of a line in the Analects of Confucius which goes *"Shi iwaku, ware jūyūgo ni shite manabu ni kokorozasu"* (子曰、吾十有五而志于学, "At fifteen, I set my heart upon learning".) So maybe Kanesada´s reason for using this wording was that he tried to give a hint that he set his heart upon learning the craft of sword forging at the age of sixteen.

Anyway, the date signature "Ansei shichi sarudoshi nigatsu jūsannichi" ("13ᵗʰ day of the second month Ansei 7 [1860], year of the monkey") does not match the production date of the blade because it was the sixth year of Kaei (嘉永, 1853) when Kanesada was 16 years old. That means the date mentions when Egami Tokurin (his first name might also read "Norichika") tested the blade on a body with a slender hipbone (*Hosogoshi*) at the consecrated testing ground (*Dotaba-rai*). But when we take a closer look at both signatures we learn that the actual *Mei* and the date of Ansei 7 go back to the same hand, i.e. to Kanesada. On the other hand, the *Mei* "Aizu-jū Kanemoto – Jūyūroku-sai saku" is executed a bit more "insecure" than the *Mei* on the *Ura* side chiselled eight years later. And this in turn points again to the fact that we are facing here a signature from the Kanesada´s earliest active period.

Kanesada started to learn sword forging from his father from Kaei 3 (1850) onwards. When he was 16 years old, i.e. at the time he made this blade, he entered on the behalf of the fief an apprenticeship as repair man of tools and implements and had in the eleventh month of the same year the honor to demonstrate his craft in front of higher officials of the fief, namely in front of the *Bugu-bugyō* (武具奉行, the arms and armors magistrate), the *Go-kanjō-gashira* (御勘定頭, the finance chief), and the *Go-metsuke-tachai* (御目付立会, the supervisor for the audiences with the *Shōgun*). He did well and received as a reward the stipend for the support of one person. Information on his age are extremely rare on Kanesada´s blades. The blade is in *Hira-zukuri*, i.e. in a shape which is relatively easy to forge, even for a swordsmith trainee, and this too points to the fact that this *Wakizashi* is truly from that time, that means from the time he demonstrated his craft and started to forge blades all by himself.

The *Kitae* is a very dense *ko-Itame* mixed with a hint of Masame and the Koyama Munetsugu-style *Hamon* shows roundish and uniform *Yakigashira*, an interpretation which is rare for Kanesada. But the *Nie* is evenly distributed (i.e. no unintended accumulations) and the tempering was excellently executed. The aforementioned interpretation of the *Hamon* might suggest that he had whatsoever contact with Koyama Munetsugu (固山宗次) or his older brother Munetoshi (宗俊) from Shirakawa (白河) which was located in the neighboring province of Mutsu. This supposed contact is further substantiated by the fact that Munetsugu´s son studied later under Kanesada. And when we take a look at the *Yasurime* at the *Nakago-jiri* we learn that they do not appear in the horizontal manner which is usual for Kanesada but in a vertical manner which in turn is typical for Koyama Munetsugu. An interesting feature which is only seen on this *Wakizashi* of Kanesada.

So we have here a very precious reference work, not only in terms of the fact that it is a work from the time Kanesada started to forge blades all by himself but also in terms of the excellent quality which shows the great talent he had at the young age of 16.

(Kawashima)

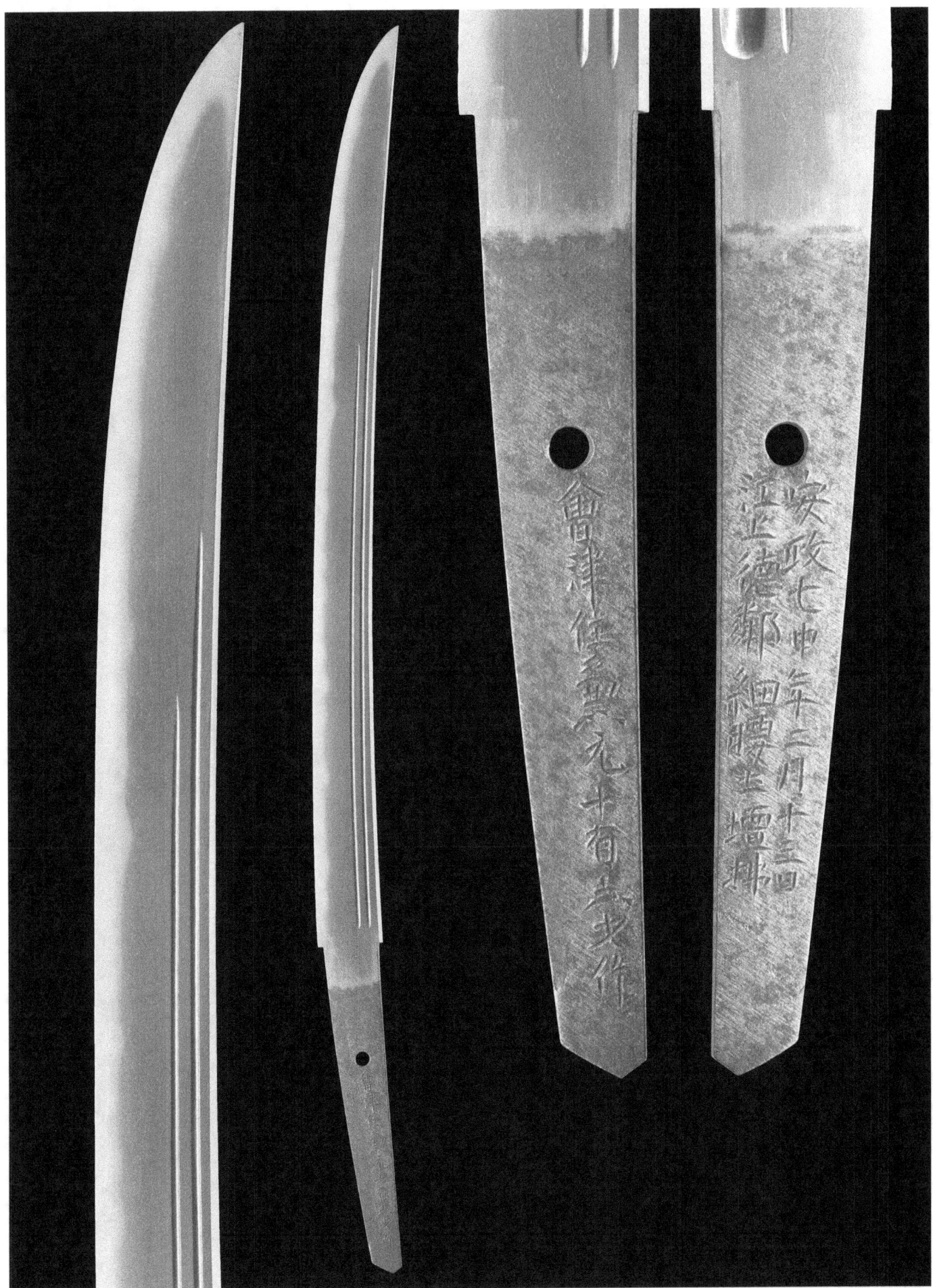

Katana

Mei:
Omote: Okushū Aizu ju Fujiwara Kanesada, Ansei 5 uma-doshi san gatsu jū-san nichi, Tōuto Senjuin (ni) oite. Ryoshabutsu dotan Yamada Genzōkore (wo) Tamesu, Ogawa Gōzaemon Mitodoke
奥州會津住藤原兼定
安政五午年三月十三日東都於千住 両車拂土壇　山田源蔵試之 小川郷左衛門見届
March 13th. At Senjuin in Tokyo the Tameshigiri was performed and the cut went along the hip bone and right into the earth. Witnessed by Ogawa Gōzaemon

Ura: Kaei 7 nen Kinoe-tora 9 gatsubi
嘉永七年甲寅九月日
A day in September [1854]

Nagasa: 2 shaku 3 sun 1 bu 4 ri (70.1 cm)
Sori: 5 bu (1.5 cm)

Jitetsu is *Masame* with *Ara-nie*, *Nie-utsuri* all over the blade, *Tobiyaki* and *Ji-nie*. *Hamon* is roundish *Sanbon-sugi* mixed with *Togariba* with *Ko-nie* which is typical Kanesada style, many *Sunagashi* and *Madara-nie* with strong *Nie*.

It is made as *Daisaku-Daimei* at Kaei 7 (1854) when 11th Kanesada was 17 years old. This is the evidence that 11th Kanesada had a talent to be a great master swordsmith when he was already 17 years old.

Regarding the person Ogawa Gōzaemon, we can find his name as 武具奉行京都詰め "an officer of the department of arms in Kyoto *150 koku*" in 慶応年間會津藩士名録（勉強堂書店出版）"The list of Aizu hanshi names in Keiō period."

It is said that Ogawa Gōzaemon left Boso area on Kaei 7 (1854) October, moved to Edo Kanansugi Jinya and worked there for five years until Ansei 7 (1860) September. So, probably, he was there as a witness to the *Tameshigiri* on that day.

(Toyama)

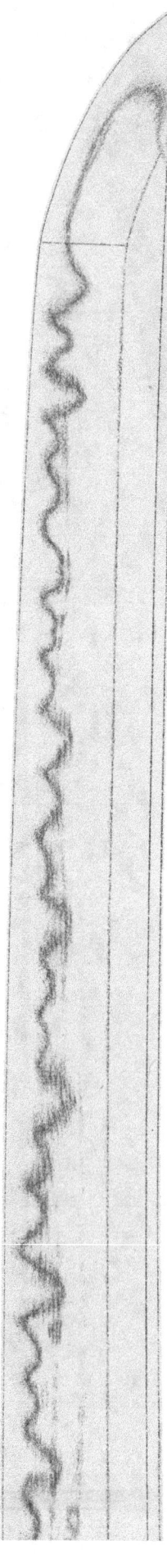

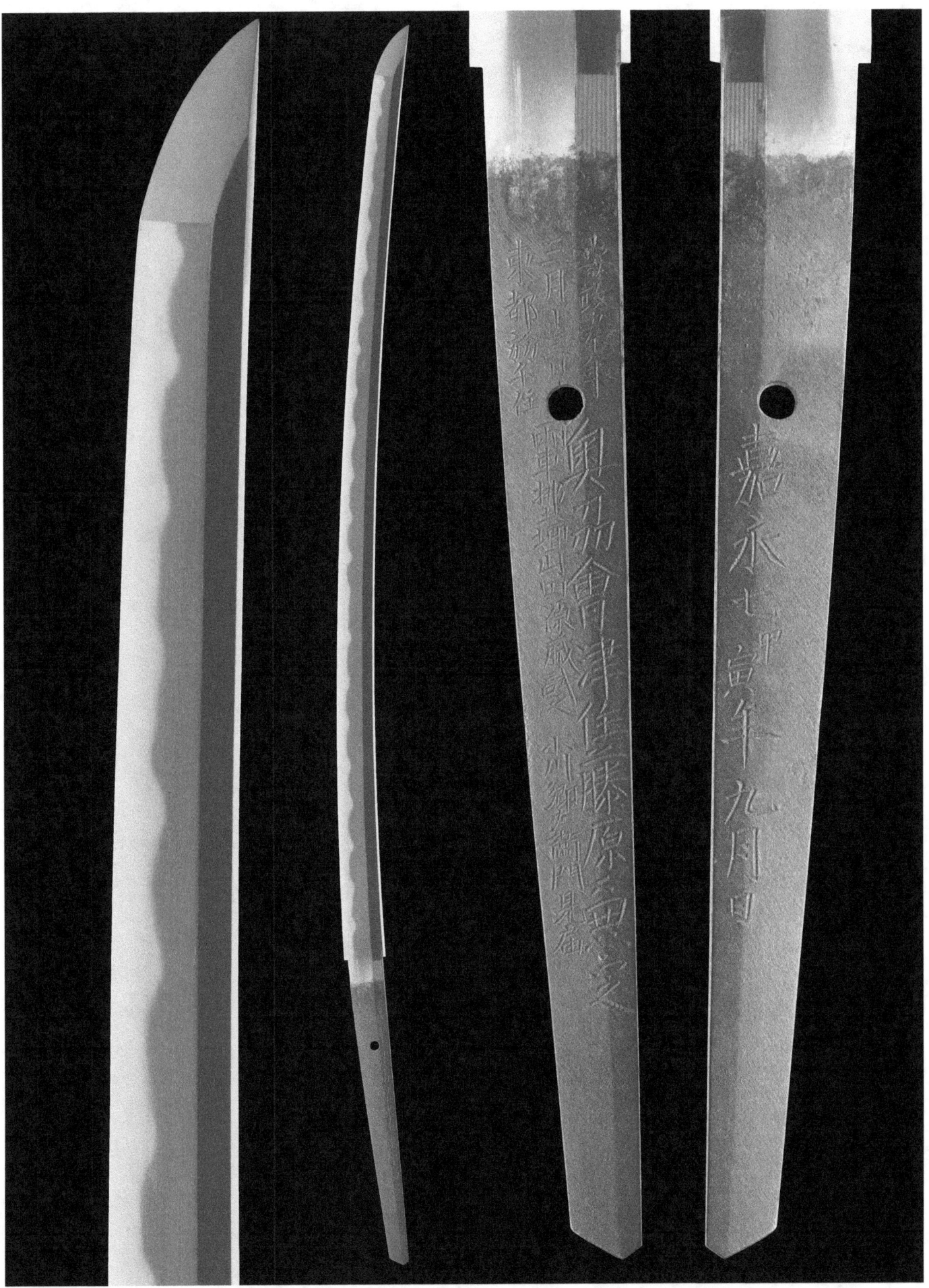

Katana

Mei:
Omote: *Aizu-shin Kanesada Kanemoto Seishin*
(wo) hikite sanmai-sei (o) motte
kore (o) tsukuru – Ansei yon hinoto
hebi-doshi hachigatsu kichijitsu
會藩臣兼定兼元・抽精神以三枚製
而造之・安政四丁巳年八月吉日
Made with special diligence and in the
Sanmai technique by the Aizu fief retainers
Kanesada and Kanemoto on a lucky day
of the eighth month Ansei 4 [1857]

Ura: *Dōnen jūichigatsu jūsannichi – Ōwakige*
hatsuba hirado itaru – Dōyō-shi
Nagasaka Katsuyasu kore o tamesu
同年十一月十三日・大脇毛初刃至
平土・同陽士長坂勝安試之
Nagakatsu Katsuyasu, a retainer from the
same fief, performed with this blade on
the 13th day of the eleventh month of
the same year a test cut at which the first cut
along the height of the armpits cut
[through the body] and right into the earth

Nagasa: 2 *shaku* 3 *sun* 1 *bu* 4 *ri* (70,1 cm)
Sori: 5 *bu* (1,5 cm)

This blade was made in Ansei 4 (1857) when Kanesada was 20 years old. It is signed with "Kanemoto" and atop with the name of his father, the 10th generation Kanesada. So we have here another highly precious reference, namely a joint work of father and son and one of the earliest time of the 11th generation Kanesada when he still signed with "Kanemoto." It is interpreted in the typical shape of Kanesada, i.e. with a normal *Mihaba* and *Kasane* in combination with a high *Shinogi*. The *Kitae* is very dense *ko-Itame* which tends a bit to *Nagare*. The *Hamon* is *chū-Suguha* in *ko-Nie-deki* with bright and tight *Nioiguchi*. The *Bōshi* is *Sugu* with *Komaru-kaeri* and the tang bears the additional information that the blade was forged in the *Sanmai-awase* technique. And the *Tameshi-mei* on the *Ura* side tesitfies to the sharpness of the blade when the Aizu-retainer Nagasaka Katsuyasu cut through the entire body at the height of the armpits and right into the earth mount on which the body was placed. Incidentally, the supplement *"Chūseishin"* (抽精神) means that the blade was made from selected highest quality raw materials and with special diligence, i.e. in a more time-consuming and sophisticated forging method.

(Kawashima)

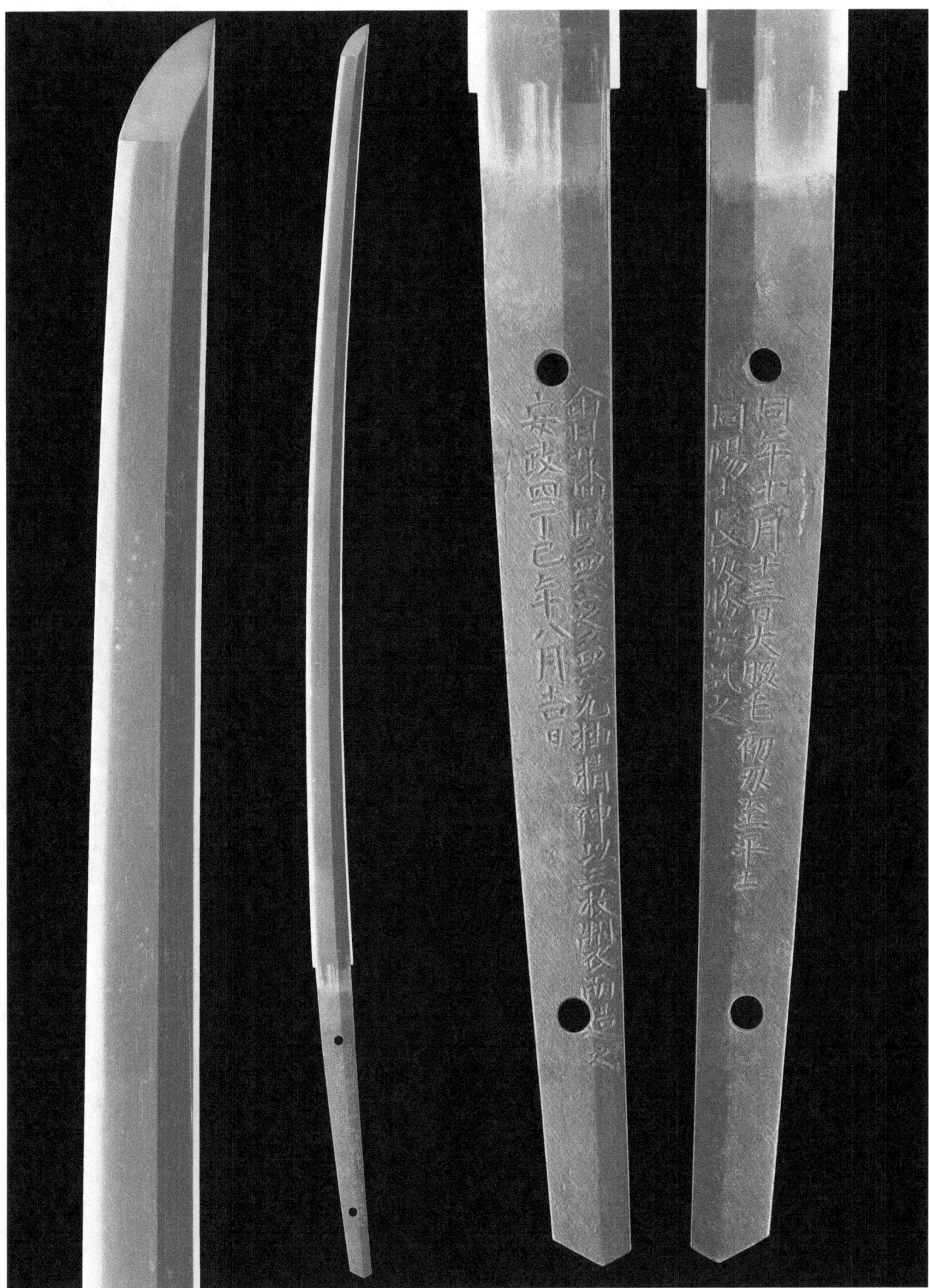

Katana:

Mei:
Omote: Mutsu Kaiyoshin Fujiwara Kanemoto
　　　　Seiriki (wo) Hikite kore (wo) tsukuru
　　　　陸奥會陽臣藤原兼元
　　　　抽精力造之
　　　　Mutsu Kaiyoshin Fujiwara Kanemoto,
　　　　made with extraction of vital energy
Ura:　Ansei 7 Kanoe-saru doshi ni gatsu Kichijitsu
　　　　安政7庚申年二月吉日
　　　　A lucky day of February, Ansei 7 [1860]
Nagasa: 2 *shaku* 3 *sun* 6 *bu* (71.5 cm)
Sori:　 1 *bu* 7 *ri* (0.5 cm)

Jitetsu is tight *ko-Mokume* (鉄冴える *Sairu*), serene steel. *Hamon* is roundish head *Sanbonsugi* in *Nie-deki* with many *Sunagashi* near *Habuchi*.

　This is a sword made when Kanesada was 24 years old Ansei 7 (1860). He was good in *Sanbonsugi-hamon* as he signed himself as Kanemoto. This sword is a typical work of his early (Kanemoto) period.

　It is signed "Seiriki (wo) Hikite kore (wo) tsukuru," which means a specially elaborated work.

(Toyama)

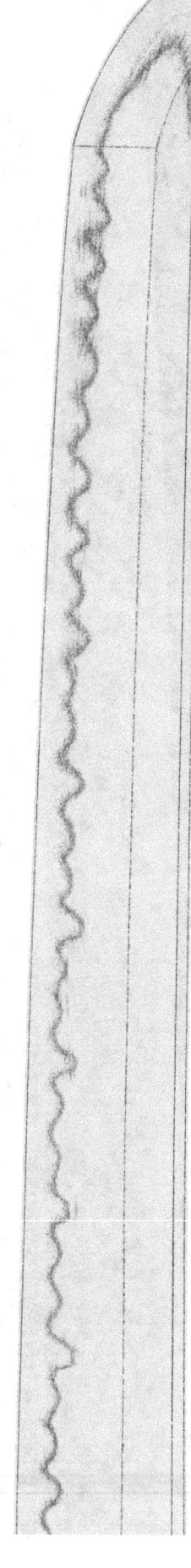

- 36 -

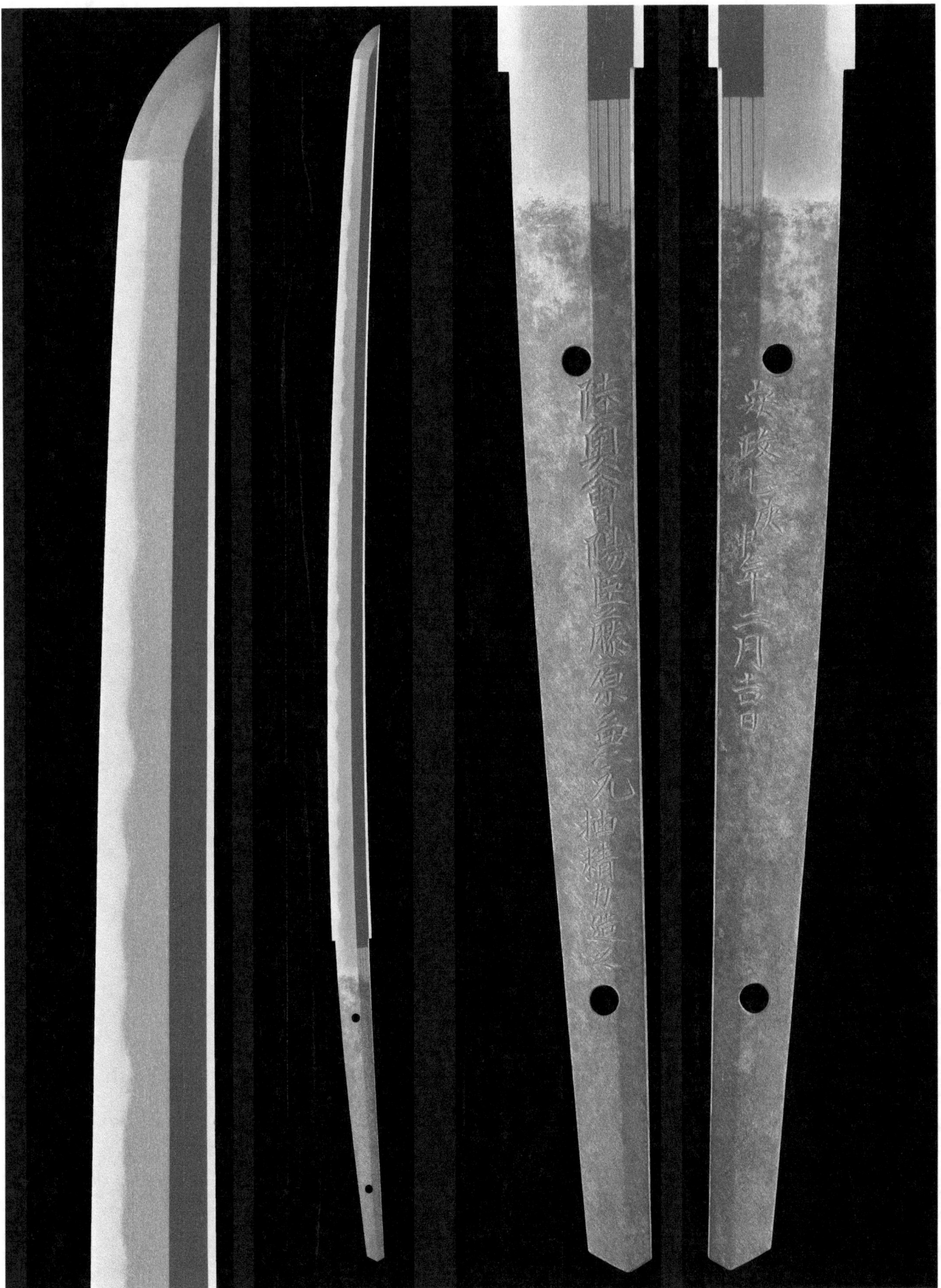

Wakizashi

Mei:
Omote: *Aizu-shin Kanemoto*
會藩臣兼元
Kanemoto, retainer of the Aizu fief
Ura: *Man'en gan sarudoshi shigatsu hi*
萬延四申年四月日
A day of the fourth month
Man'en 1 [1860], year of the monkey
Nagasa: 1 *shaku* 2 *sun* 4 *bu* (37,6 cm)
Sori: 3 *bu* 6 *ri* (1,1 cm)

This *Wakizashi* is interpreted in a *Kotō naginata-naoshi* style what is rare for Kanesada. The *Jigane* is *Masame* with *Chikei* and *Ji-nie* and the *Hamon* is *Gunome* with uniform *Yakigashira* which is periodically mixed with larger *Gunome* elements. The tempering is in *Nie-deki* and relative *Nie*-loaden and we see many thick *Ashi* and *Sunagashi*. The *Nioiguchi* is wide and bright.

The blade is signed "Kanemoto" and was thus made before he received the honorary title "Izumi no Kami" and the *Ura* side is dated Man'en 1 (1860).

(Kawashima)

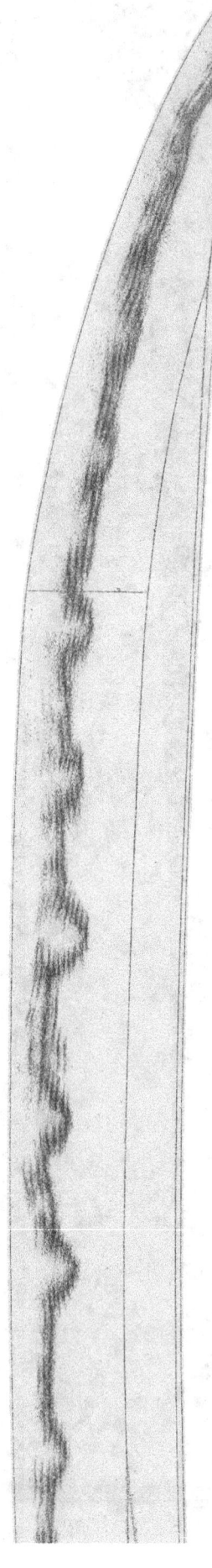

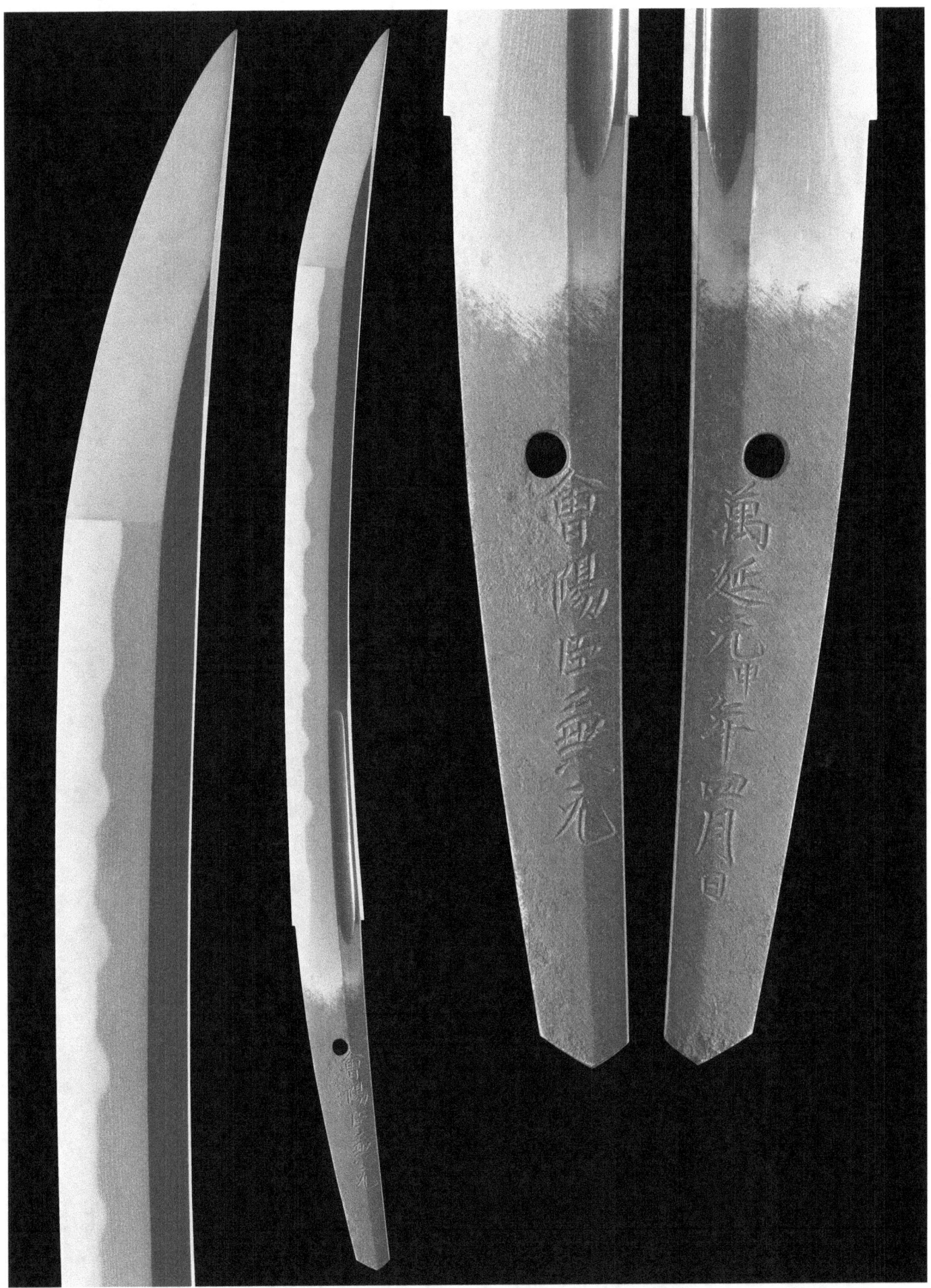

Tantō

Mei:
Omote: *Aiyō-shin Kanemoto kore o tsukuru – Bunkyū gan kanoto-toridoshi hachigatsu kichijitsu*
會陽臣兼元造之・文久元辛酉年八月吉日
A lucky day of the eighth month
Bunkyū 1 [1861], year of the rooster
Ura: *Kimibanzai*
君萬歳
Long Life for the Sovereign
Nagasa: *9 sun 3 bu* (28,2 cm)
Sori: *1 bu 5 ri* (0,45 cm)

This blade bears the early signature "Kanemoto" and is dated Bunkyū 1 (1861) when Kanesada was 25 years old. *Sugata* is *Hira-zukuri* and *Sunnobi* with shallow *Sori*. The *Kitae* is *Mokume* mixed with *Itame* which shows partially also some *ō-Hada*. The *Hamon* is a *Kotō* Kanemitsu-like (兼光) *Gunome* mixed with *Togariba* and plentiful of *Sunagashi* and *Kinsuji* and *Inazuma* in the *Monouchi* area, i.e. we see a vivid and varied *Ha* which emulates *Kotō* works. The *Bōshi* tends to *Jizō* and has a long *Kaeri*. Incidentally, the term "Kimibanzai" on the *Ura* side of the *Nakago* refers to wishes for a long life of the *Shōgun* or the family of the *Shōgun* respectively.

(Kawashima)

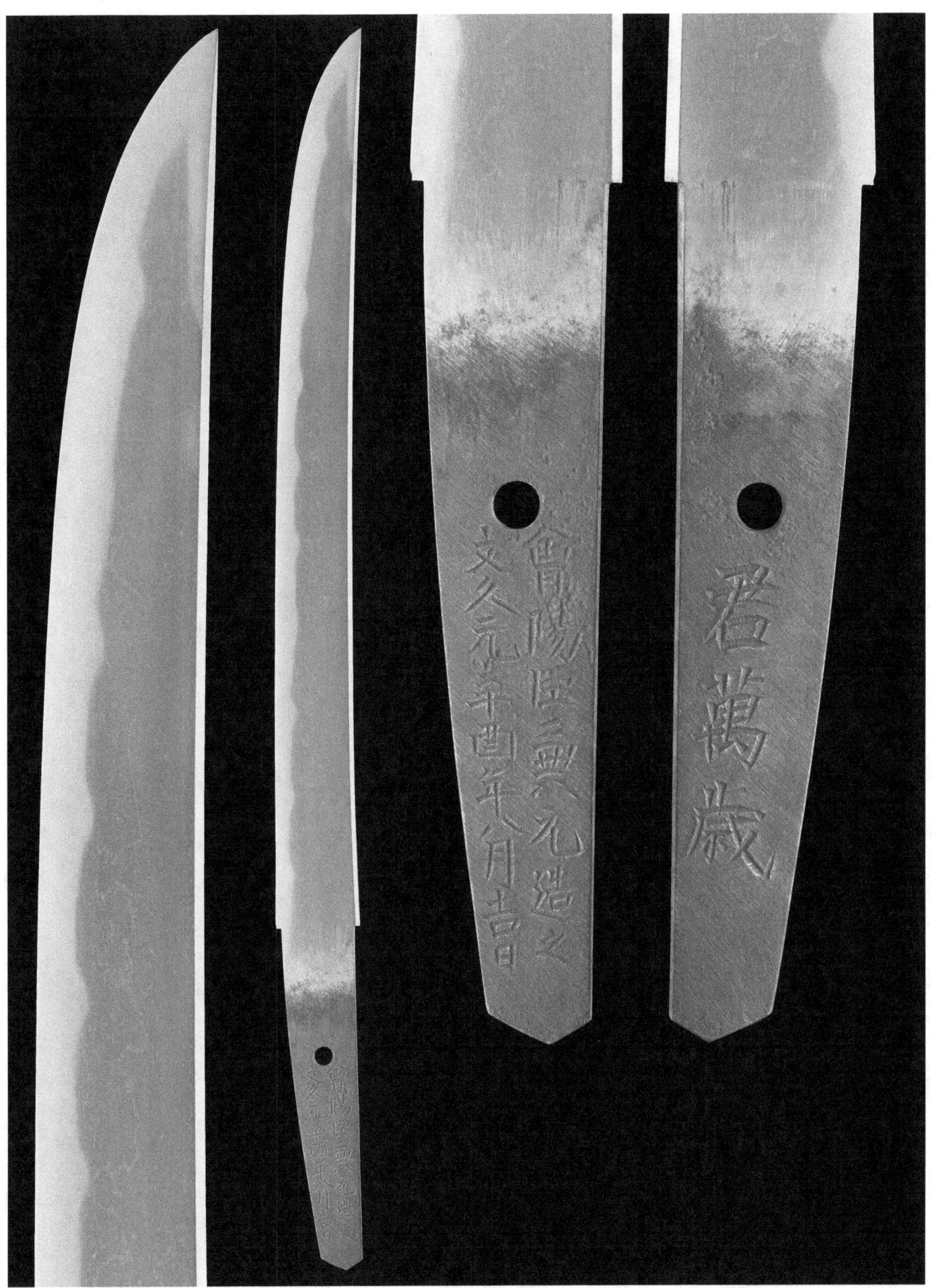

Katana:

Mei:
Omote: *Aizu-jū Kanemoto – Kyōsen no toki juryō – Izumi no Kami Kanesada gō*
會津住兼元・京戦之時受領・和泉守兼定号
Kanemoto from Aizu who received the honorary title Izumi no Kami whilst staying in Kyōto in time of war – [Now] called Kanesada

Ura: *Okada Yasumitsu no tame Yasuhide no okuru ni saku – Kimibanzai – Keiō gan ushidoshi jūgatsu yokka – Hatsu ninodō tameshi Yasuhide*
為岡田安光安秀送作・君萬歳・慶應元丑年十月四日・初二ノ胴試安秀
Sent on behalf of Okada Yasumitsu to Yasuhide – Long Life for the Sovereign – On the fourth day of the tenth month Keiō 1 [1865]. First test by Yasuhide via a second body cut

Nagasa: 2 *shaku* 3 *sun* 3 *bu* 6 *ri* (70,8 cm)
Sori: 5 *ri* (1,5 cm)

The blade measures a little over 70 cm and has a *Sori* of 1,5 cm, that means we are facing here one of the deeper curved blades known by Kanesada. Anyway, the *Mihaba* is normally wide and the *Sugata* is excellent. The *Kitae* is a very dense *ko-Itame* with a little *Masame* towards the *Ha*. *Ji-nie* appears and the steel is bright. The *Hamon* is a *chū-Suguha* in *ko-Nie-deki* with a very tight *Nioiguchi*, *Nijūba*-like elements and partially quite emphasized *Nie* which appear in *Yubashiri* manner parallel to the *Ha*.

The inscription on the *Nakago* makes this blade a very important reference but is also highly interesting. It is mentioned that he made it when he was in Kyōto and when there was a war. As we know, he received his honorary title "Izumi no Kami" in the twelfth month of Bunkyū 3 (文久, 1863) so it is assumed that the supplement "in time of war" refers to the Hamaguri Gate Rebellion which took place in the seventh month of the subsequent year, i.e. Bunkyū 4 (= Genji 1). Without a doubt, the entire inscription was done by Kanesada himself, but we can see a few differences in the strength of the chiselling and the rust at the very bottom of the chisel strokes. So we learn that the parts of the signature were added at different times. Also we learn that a certain Okada Yasumitsu ordered Kanesada to send this sword to Okada Yasuhide, probably his son, and that the latter performed with it his first test cut in Keiō 1, i.e. about two years after the blade was made. That means the most likely scenario is that Okada Yasuhide – the new owner of the blade – asked Kanesada to add the other info like his first test cut and that the master bears now the title "Izumi no Kami" and the name "Kanesada" to the tang after Kanesada´s return to Aizu in the very same year.

(Kawashima)

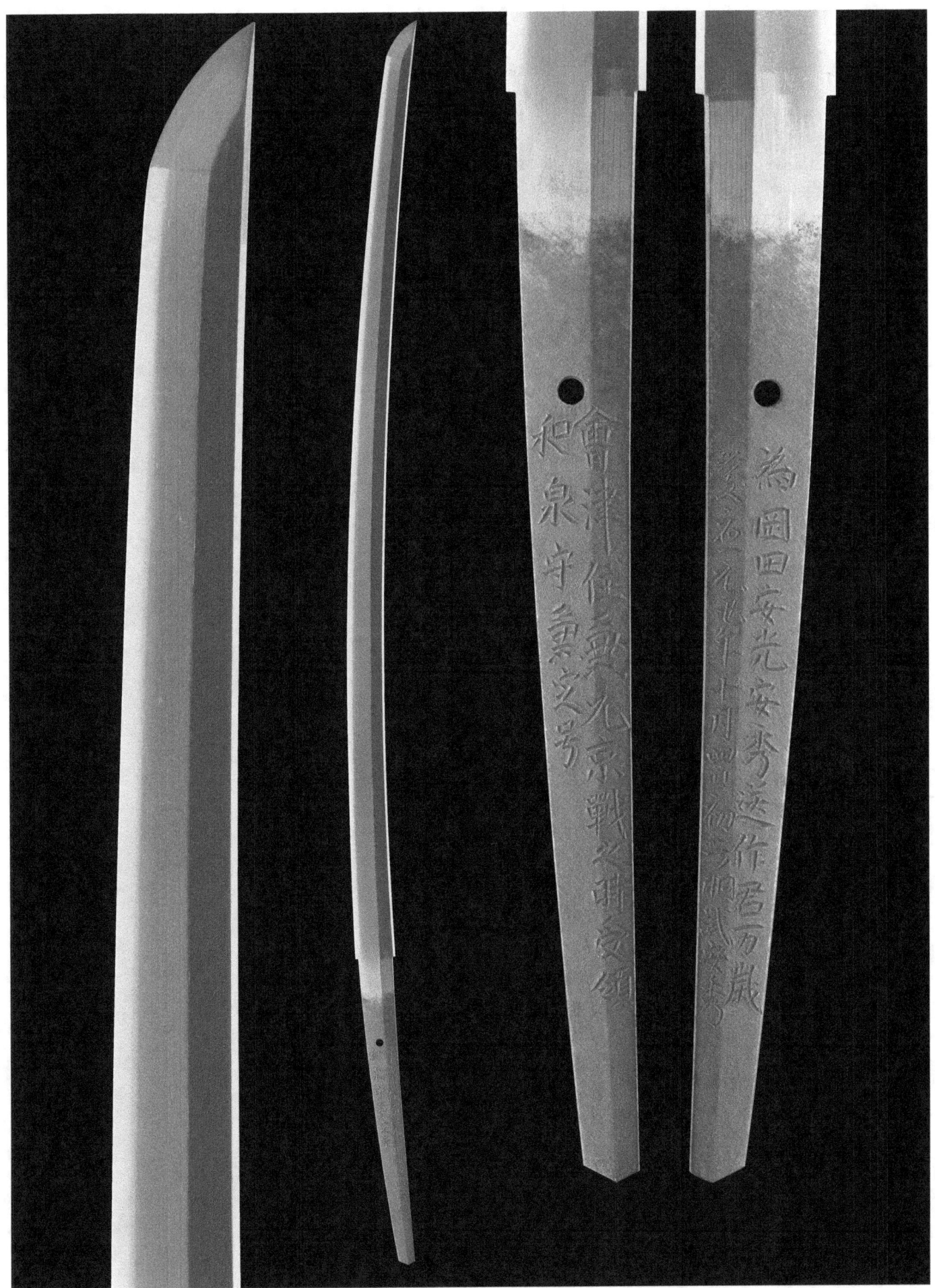

Katana

Mei: *Aiyō-shi – Izumi no Kami Kanesada*
         會陽士・和泉守兼定
         Izumi no Kami Kanesada,
         retainer of the Aizu fief
Nagasa: 2 *shaku* 4 *sun* 7 *bu* 5 *ri* (75,0 cm)
Sori: 5 *bu* 3 *ri* (1,6 cm)

As for the *Sugata*, the blade does not taper that much, has a thick *Kasane*, and an elongated tip, i.e. an *ō-Kissaki*. The *Jigane* is a *ko-Mokume* mixed with *Masame* and the *Hamon* is *Chōji* mixed with *Gunome*. The *Gunome* part in turn tends to *Sanbonsugi* and *Nie* appears. The *Bōshi* has a deep *Kaeri* which connects with the *Muneyaki* and there are some *Tobiyaki*.

Such a magnificent *Shinshintō-Sugata* with a large and elongated *Kissaki* is rare for Kanesada. The blade is undated but we can see certain peculiarities in the execution of the character for "Kane" (兼). The inner part of the character shows the radical (艹) as seen in detail ※1. This interpretation is typical for his earlier active period when he signed with "Kanemoto" until shortly after receiving the honorary title "Izumi no Kami" and changing his name to "Kanesada." After his return from Kyōto to Aizu, i.e. from the Keiō era (慶応, 1865-1868) onwards, he executed this inner part with the radical (寸) as seen in detail ※2. For example, the *Mei* "Kanemoto" of the previous blade is signed in the former interpretation of the character for "Kane", and the supplement "Kanesada" in the latter interpretation, what underlines once more the aforementioned scenario of how the inscription has to be understood. In short, this blade was made right after he had received his honorary title, and it is thus one of the rare extant works from his stay in Kyōto.

(Kawashima)

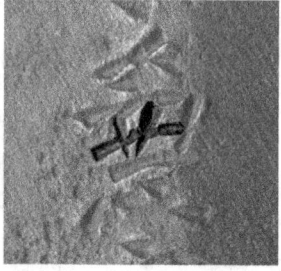

※1

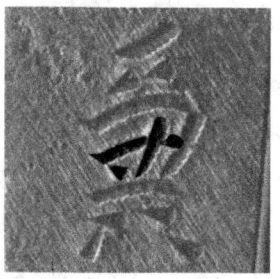

※2

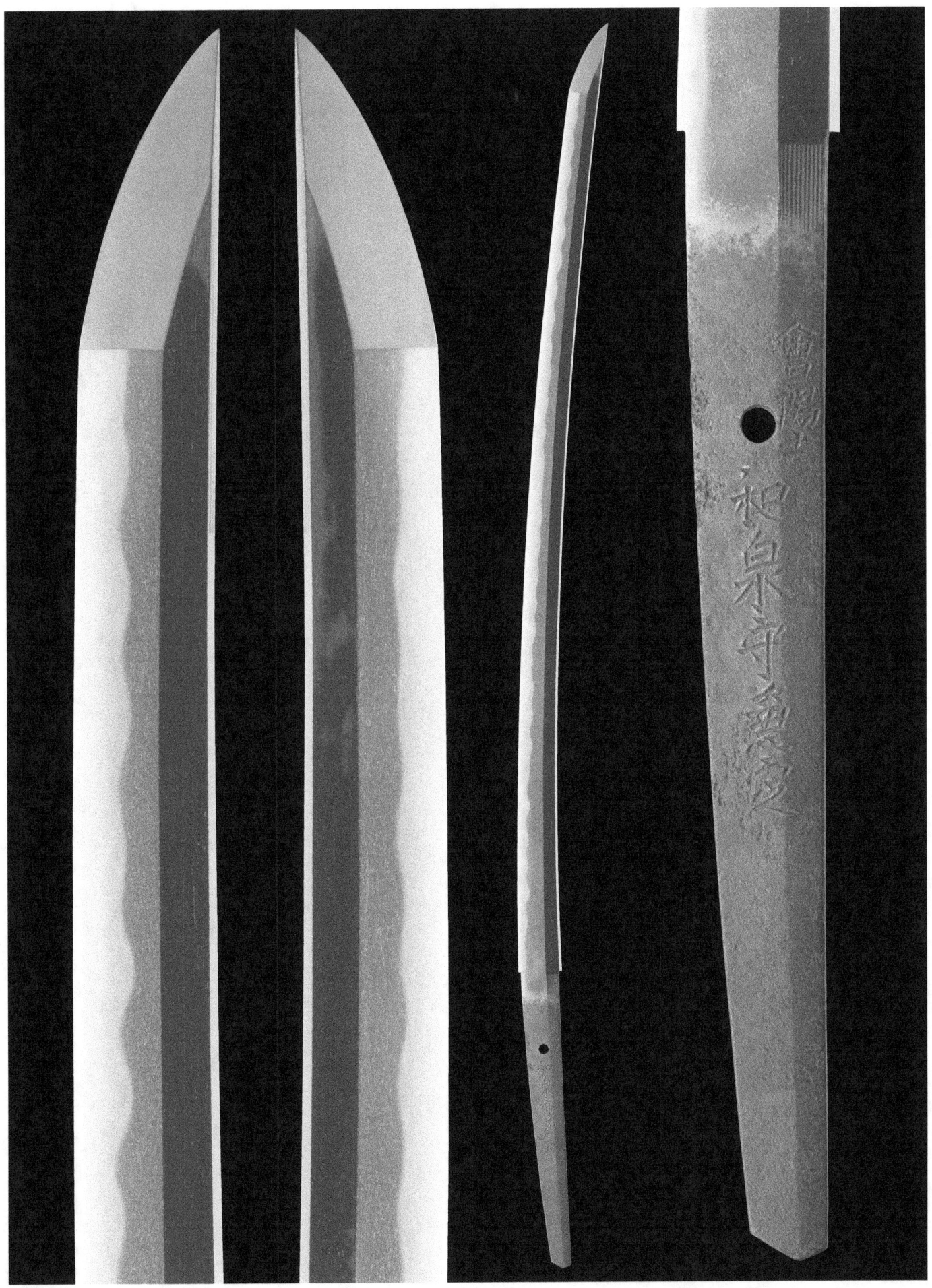

Katana

Mei:
Omote: Izumi no Kami Fujiwara Ason Kanesada
和泉守藤原朝臣兼定
Ura: Keiō Gan Ushi-doshi hachi gatsu bi
慶応元年丑年八月日
A day of August, Keiō Gan-nen
[1865], in the year of the ox
Nagasa: 2 shaku 4 sun 5 bu (74.2 cm)
Sori: 5 bu (1.5 cm)

Jitetsu is very tight *ko-Mokume*, almost *Muji Hada*, *Hamon* is *Gunome* mixed with *Togariba* intensely *Midare*, *Nijuba* with bright *Nie* all over the blade.

This is the work of Keiō Gan-nen (1865). It is one of the most wild *Hamon* of his work which made us imagine that Kanesada tried *Soshu-den*.

The highlight of this sword is strong *Nie* of *Soshu-den* with *Togariba* of *Mino-den*.

It was owned by a private collector in Niigata and it has been said to be one of the best masterpieces of his work. It has a very strong *Sugata*, the length is longer and wider than average of his work.

(Toyama)

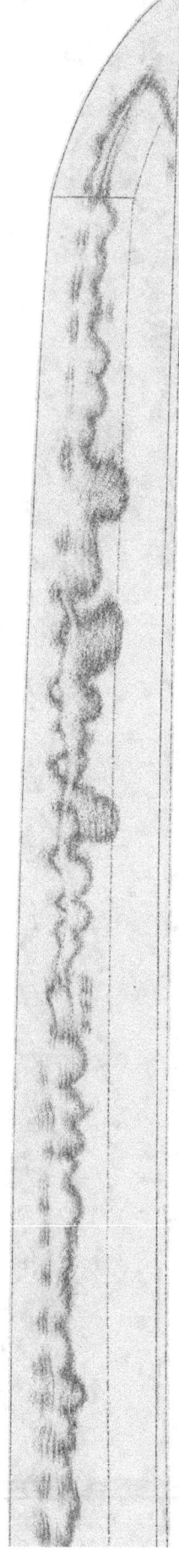

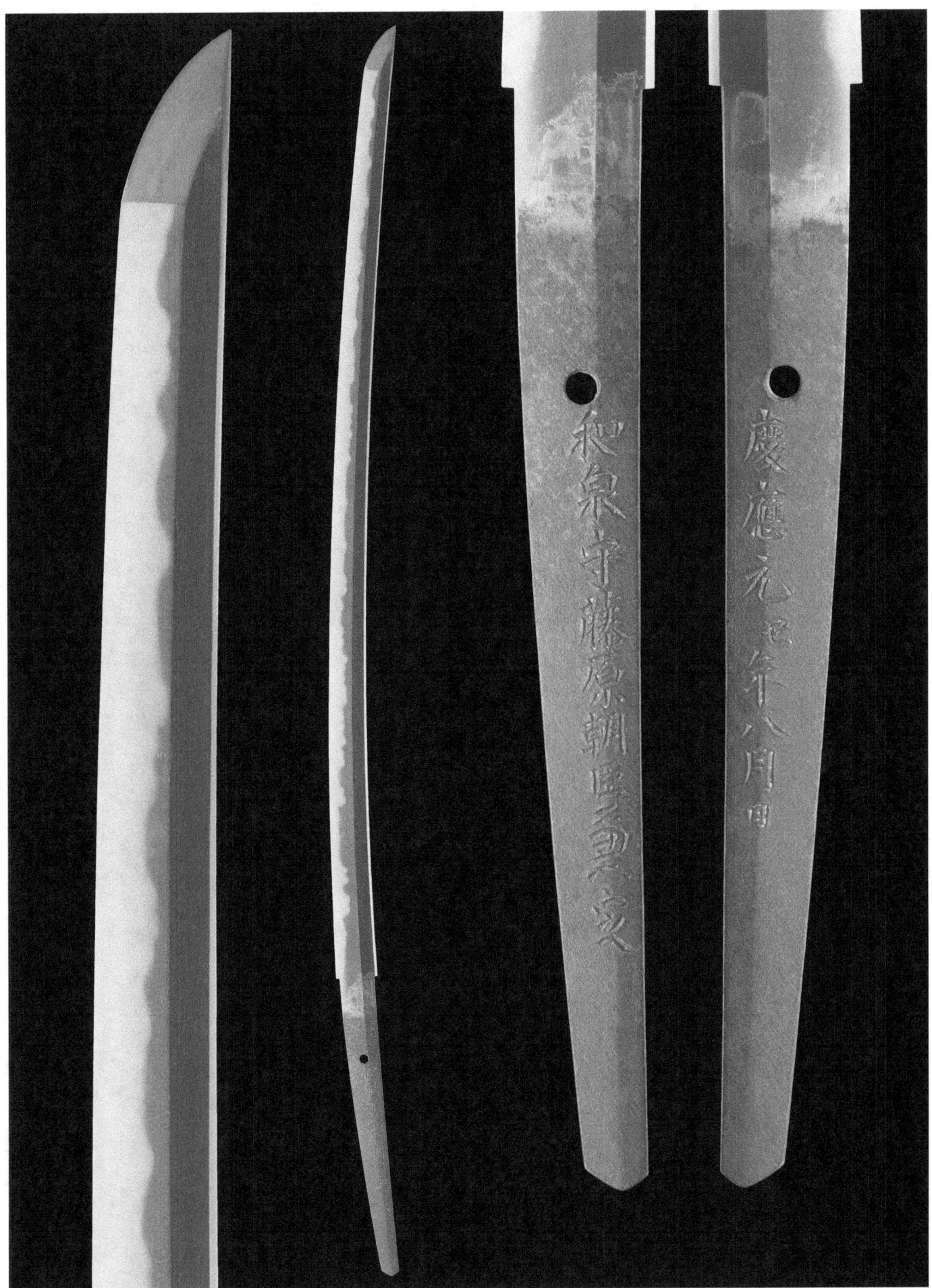

Katana

Mei:
Omote: *Izumi no Kami Fujiwara Ason Kanesada*
和泉守藤原朝臣兼定
Ura: *Keiō 2 tora-doshi 8 gatsu bi*
慶応二寅年八月日
A day of August, Keiō 2
[1866], the year of the tiger
Nagasa: *2 shaku 3 Sun 1 Bu* (69.9 cm)
Sori: *5 Bu* (1.5 cm)

Jitetsu is *Masame* with *Nie Utsuri* and *Ji-nie* followed by *Masame*. *Hamon* is *Suguha*, with strong *Nie*, especially above the *Monouchi* even stronger *Nie*. *Jitetsu* of Kanesada most of the time has tight *Mokume*, *Masame* and *ō-Itame*. This sword is one of them with very fine and tight *Masame-kitae*. The shape is ordinary and well balanced *Sori*. This is one of the Kanesada's typical work with it's gentle shape.

(Toyama)

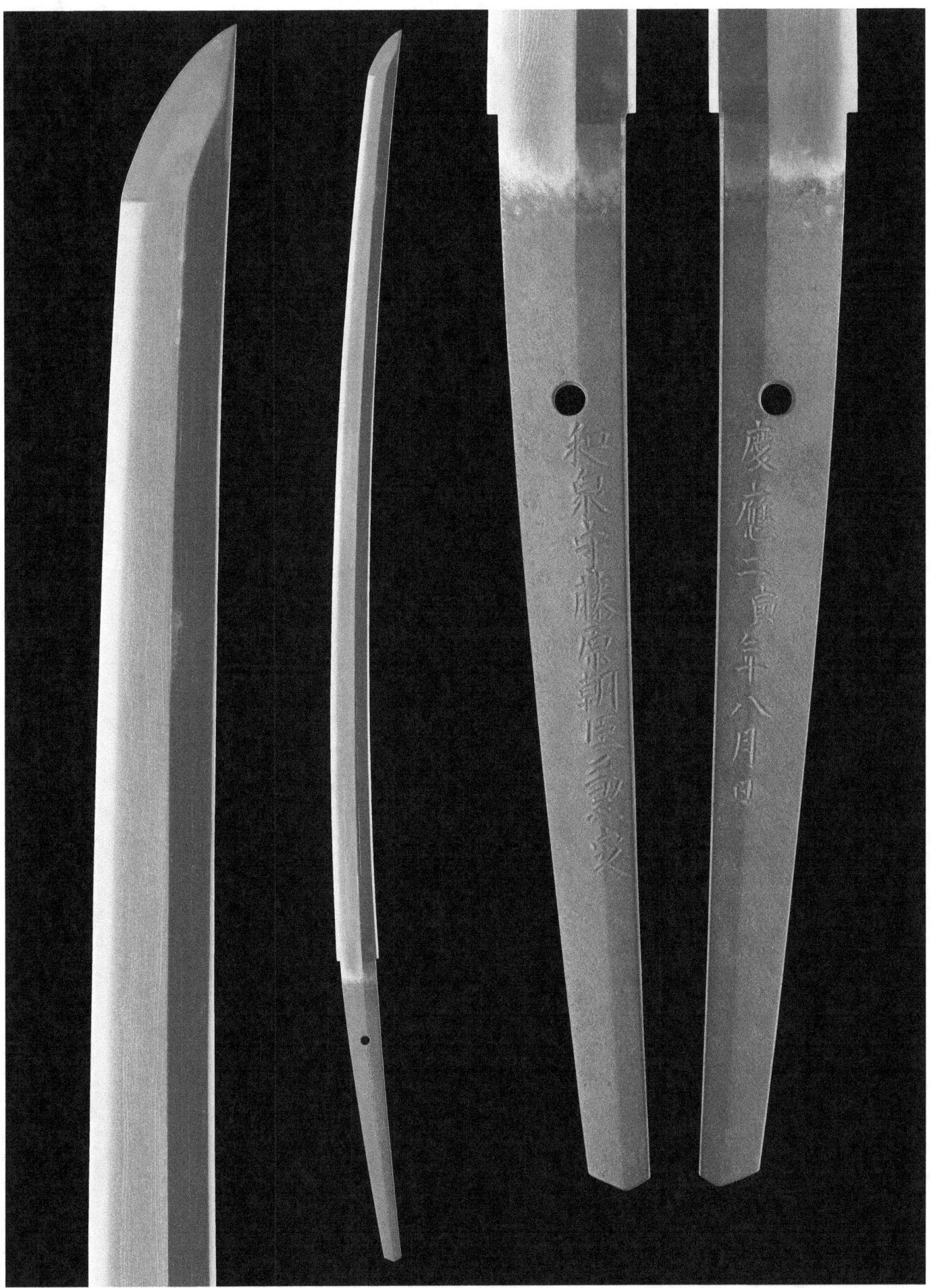

Katana

Mei:
Omote: *Izumi no Kami Kanesada*
和泉守兼定
Ura: *Keiō sannen nigatsu hi*
慶應三年二月日
A day of the second month Keiō 3 [1867]
Nagasa: 2 *shaku* 3 *sun* 1 *bu* (70,0 cm)
Sori: 4 *bu* (1,2 cm)

This *Katana* was once worn by the Shinsengumi vice-commander Hijikata Toshizō and was made one year before Toshizō's death. As Kanesada was already back in Aizu at that time, it is likely that the blade was presented to Toshizō by the Aizu fief. There is a letter of the Shinsengumi commander Kondō Isami to Toshizō's brother-in-law Satō Hikogorō from the first year of Genji (元治, 1864) extant in which Isami states that Hijikata is doing well and that he wears a *Katana* of Izumi no Kami Kanesada measuring *2 Shaku 8 Sun* (84,8 cm) and a *Wakizashi* of Horikawa Kunihiro (堀川国広) which measures *1 Shaku 9 Sun 5 Bu* (59,1 cm). And as the *Nagasa* of this blade differs, we know that Toshizō owned at least two Katana made by Kanesada.

The *Kitae* bases on a tightly forged *ko-Itame* but shows all over also *Masame*. There is plentiful of *Ji-nie* and the steel is bright. The *Hamon* is a *Sanbonsugi* which is modelled on *Kotō*-era Kanemoto interpretations, but with more uniform *Yakigashira* and not so much lively ups and downs as it is the case at Magoroku Kanemoto (孫六兼元). The tempering is in *ko-Nie-deki* and the *Nioiguchi* is bright and the *Monouchi* area does not show a *Sanbonsugi* but a Mino-like *Togariba*-based *Gunome*. Compared to the other blades shown in this publication, this one lost obviously some substance at the *Monouchi* and there are also some traces of Hijikata Toshizō's intensive use of the blade. Until the early Shōwa era the blade still showed the original *Ha-kobore* of that time but was later polished.

The *Katana* comes with a late Edo-period *Uchigatana-koshirae*. The *Saya* is lacquered in a quite reddish brown with an *Ishime* finish and different black lacquer accentuations of peonies and phoenixes and is equipped with a metal *Kojiri* to reinforce this area. All fittings are of iron and undecorated. The *Menuki* show Japanese pepper (*Sanshō*, 山椒) on a branch. The hilt wrapping is of a thin black cord leaving small *Hishi* diamonds, a *Tsukamaki* style which was popular in the *Bakumatsu* era. The *Tsukamaki* shows wear which is said to go back to Toshizō himself. The *Tsuba* is of iron and shows mulberry leaves and poem cards, an arrangement which alludes to the Tanabata (七夕) Festival of the Weaver. Tanabata is celebrated on the seventh day of the seventh month and people celebrate this day by writing wishes, sometimes in the form of poetry, on differently colored *Tanzaku* poem cards and hanging them on mulberry leaves.

Like the blade also the *Saya* shows wear and several damages which seem to go back to actual battlefield use, but of special interest is the quite obvious and partial wear of the *Tsukamaki*. From these areas of wear we learn that Toshizō grasped the hilt pretty firmly with both hands close to the *Fuchi*, excerting force especially on the thumb and index finger of both hands to form a firm grip and to hold the sword safely in both arms.

(Kawashima)

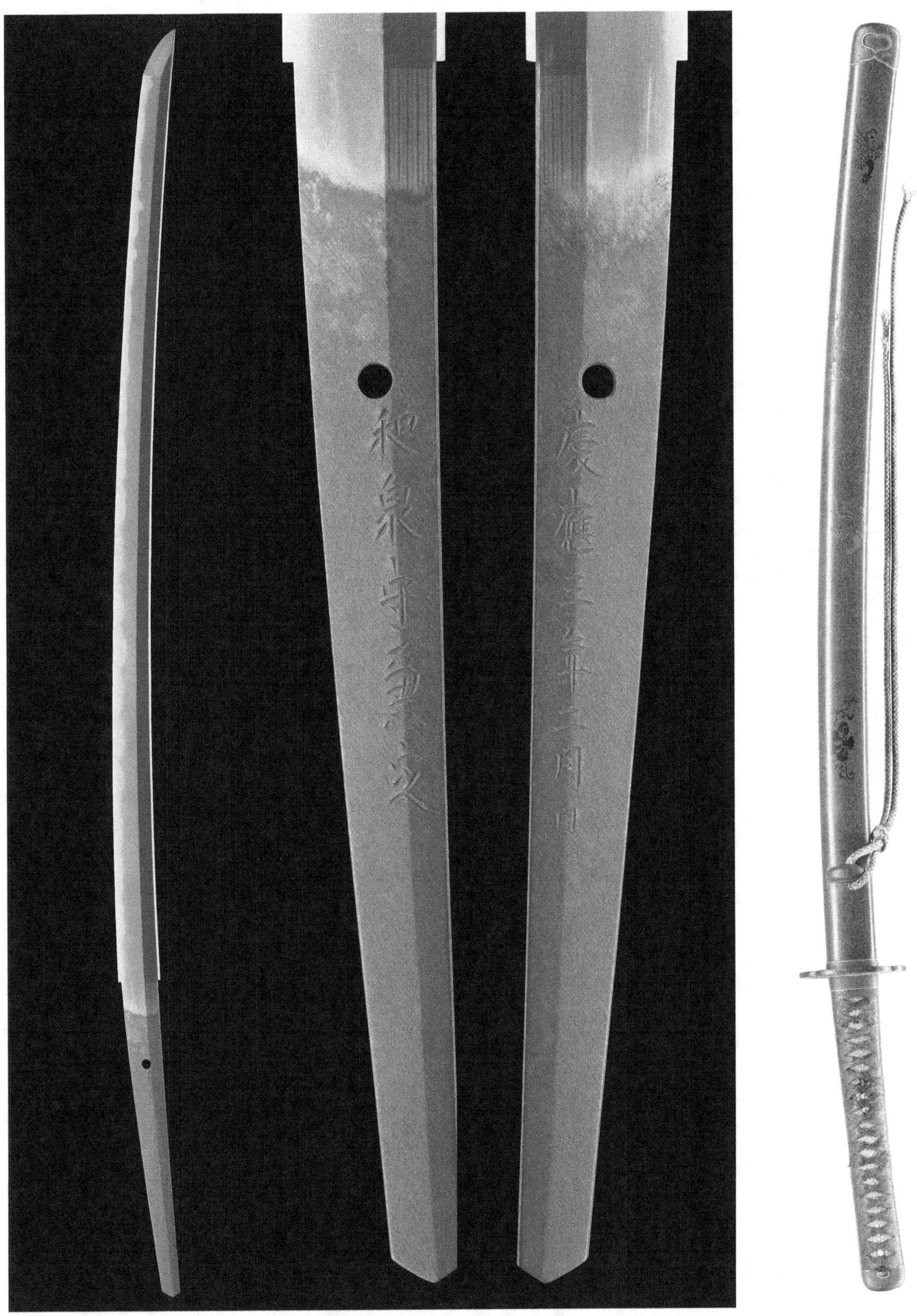

Katana

Mei:
Omote: Izumi no Kami Fujiwara Ason Kanesada
和泉守藤原朝臣兼定
Ura: Keiō san usagi-doshi ni gatsu bi
慶応三卯年二月日
A day of February, Keiō 3 [1867],
the year of the rabbit
Nagasa: 2 shaku 2 Sun 5 bu (68.1 cm)
Sori: 4 Bu (1.2 cm)

Most of the Kanesada's work has tapered gentle shape however this sword has wide *Mihaba* and not tapered, less *Sori*, thick *Kasane* and it is heavy. *Kissaki* is stretched *chū-Kissaki*. It makes strong *Sugata*.

Jitetsu is *Hadamono* and rough *Masame* near *Ha*. It becomes *ō-Itame* towards to *Shinogi* and *Shinogi-ji* is *Masame*. *Hamon* is strong *ō-Notare* with *Nie* in *Habuchi* and many fine *Kinsuji*. The speciality of Kanesada *Jitetsu* which is *Itame-hada* with *Masame* near *Ha* with *ō-Notare Hamon* we can find often in *Tantō* but *Katana* is very rare.

(Toyama)

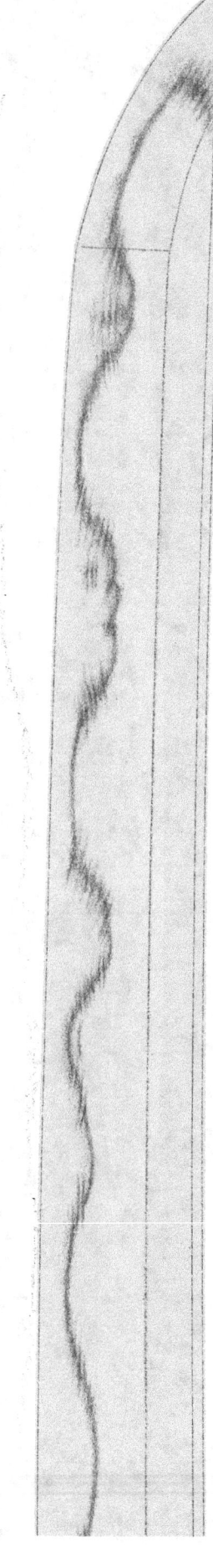

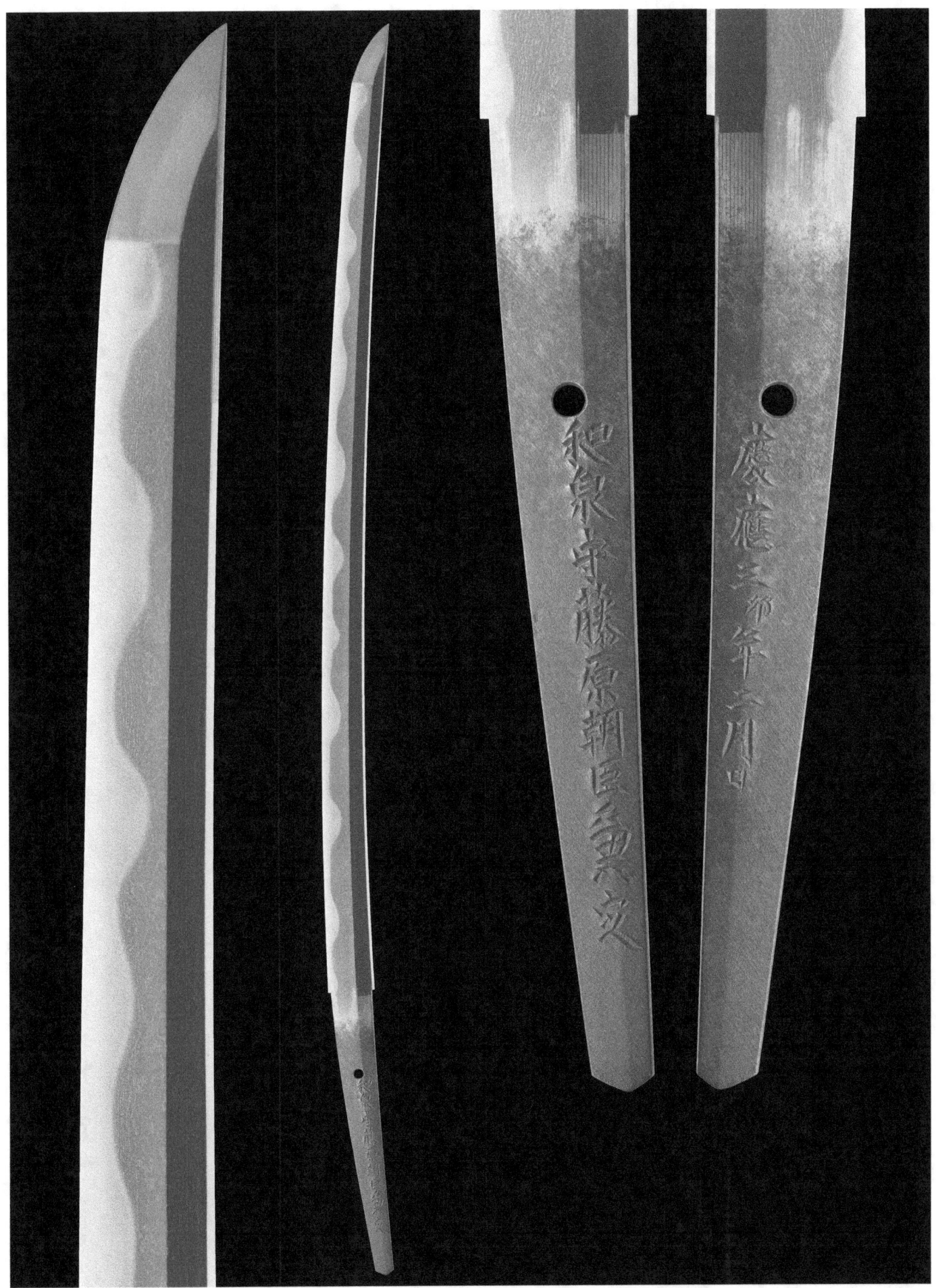

Katana

Mei:
Omote: *Mutsu-shi Izumi no Kami Fujiwara Ason Kanesada – Dōnen kugatsu nijūshichinichi Senju ni oite – Ryōguruma dotanbarai – Kirite Yamada Genzō*
陸奥士和泉守藤原朝臣兼定・同年九月二十七日於千住・両車土壇拂・切手山田源蔵
Retainer from Mutsu, Izumi no Kami Fujiwara Ason Kanesada –Yamada Genzō tested this blade on the 27th day of the ninth month of the same year via a *Ryōguruma* cut on the consecrated test ground at Senju

Ura: *Keiō san Kishima Jūhei no tame – Chūtanrensei – Dōnen dōgetsu dōjitsu dōsho ni oite – Futatsudō dotanbarai – Kirite Kishima Yūtarō*
慶應三為木嶋重平・抽鍛錬精・同年同月同日於同所・二ツ胴土壇拂・切手木嶋勇太郎
Forged with special effort in Keiō 3 [1867] for Kishima Shigehira Jūhei – Kishima Yūtarō tested this blade on the same day of the same month of the same year at the same place via a *Futatsudō* cut on the same consecrated test ground

Nagasa: 2 *shaku* 6 *sun* 5 *bu* (80,3 cm)
Sori: 4 *bu* 3 *ri* (1,3 cm)

The 11th generation Kanesada was 30 years old when he made this *Katana* in Keiō 3 (1867). From the inscription on the tang we learn that Yamada Genzō (the 8th generation Yamada Asa´emon, 山田浅右衛門) performed in Edo´s Senju on the ninth month of that year a test cut, and that the blade was once more tested on the very same day by Kishima Yūtarō. This is one of the longest blades of Kanesada extant today, but is of an outstanding quality.

The *Moto-kasane* measures almost 1 cm and the blade is in pristine condition, i.e. it shows the *Sugata* as it left the forge of the smith. As for the workmanship, it is tempered in the Kanesada-typical *Sanbonsugi*-based *Gunome* with a wide and bright *Nioiguchi* and the supplement "*Chūtanrensei*" (抽鍛錬精) means that the blade was made from selected highest quality raw materials and with special diligence, i.e. in a more time-consuming and sophisticated forging method. The blade shows a very dense *Itame* with plentiful of *Ji-nie* and partially with some fine, but strong *Chikei*, an interpretation which is atypical for the *Shinshintō* era. Details on the commissioner Kishima Jūhei are unclear, but as the second sword tester Kishima Yūtarō was a retainer of the Aizu fief it is possible that both were from the same family. And the fact that the blade is quite magnificent for a Kanesada suggests that they had – as clients – a strong influence on the smith. But when the hilt is mounted to the blade, it feels despite its length perfectly balanced what is so typical for Kanesada.

The *Katana* comes with an *Uchigatana*-style *Handachi-koshirae,* but it is hard to imagine that such a long and heavy blade was worn thrusted through the *Obi*. It is also possible that it was intended to be worn on back. A support for this approach is the fact that the *Saya* is covered with leather and reinforced by multiple layers of lacquer along its central part and the traces of wear at the two leather *Ashi-kanamono* hangers.

(Kawashima)

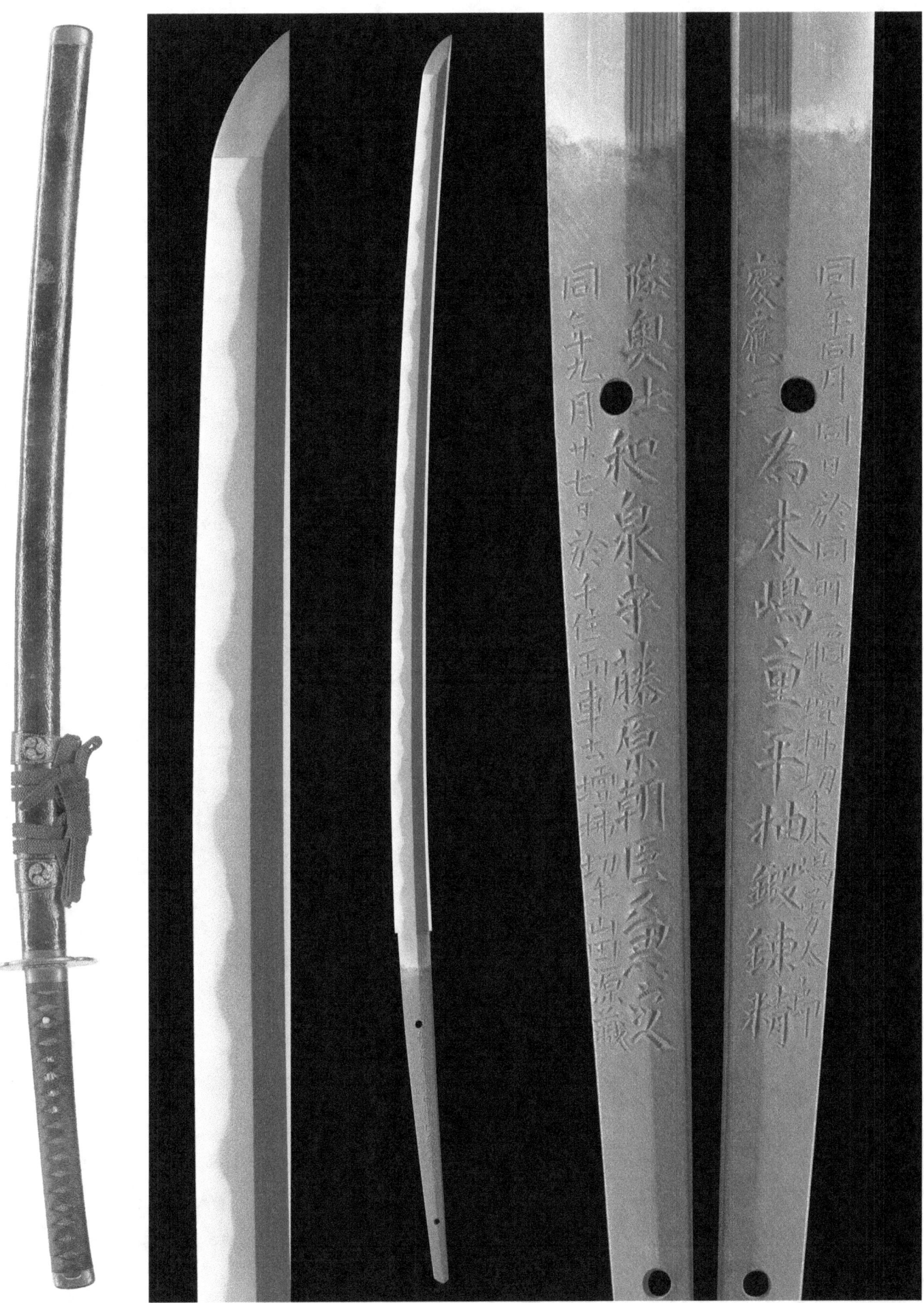

Katana

Mei:
Omote: *Aihanshi Izumi no Kami*
　　　　Fujiwara Ason Kanesada
　　　　會藩士　和泉守藤原朝臣兼定
Ura:　 *Keiō san hino-tō-doshi hachi gatsu bi*
　　　　慶応三年卯年八月日
　　　　A day of August, Keiō 3 [1867]
Nagasa:　2 *shaku* 3 *sun* (69.7 cm)
Sori:　　5 *bu* 6 *ri* (1.67 cm)

The shape of Kanesada sword is usually tapered, with a narrower *Sakihaba* and wider *Motohaba*, however this sword has wider *Sakihaba* therefor it has a strong shape. *Jitetsu* is *ō-Itame*, *Hadamono*. *Hamon* is *chū-Suguha* in *Niedeki*. We sometimes see this type of work and this is the masterpiece of his *ō-Itamehada* sword. All of the signatures in this period contain "Ason" which is cut for the elaborated works. This sword is one of them and it is very well done.

(Toyama)

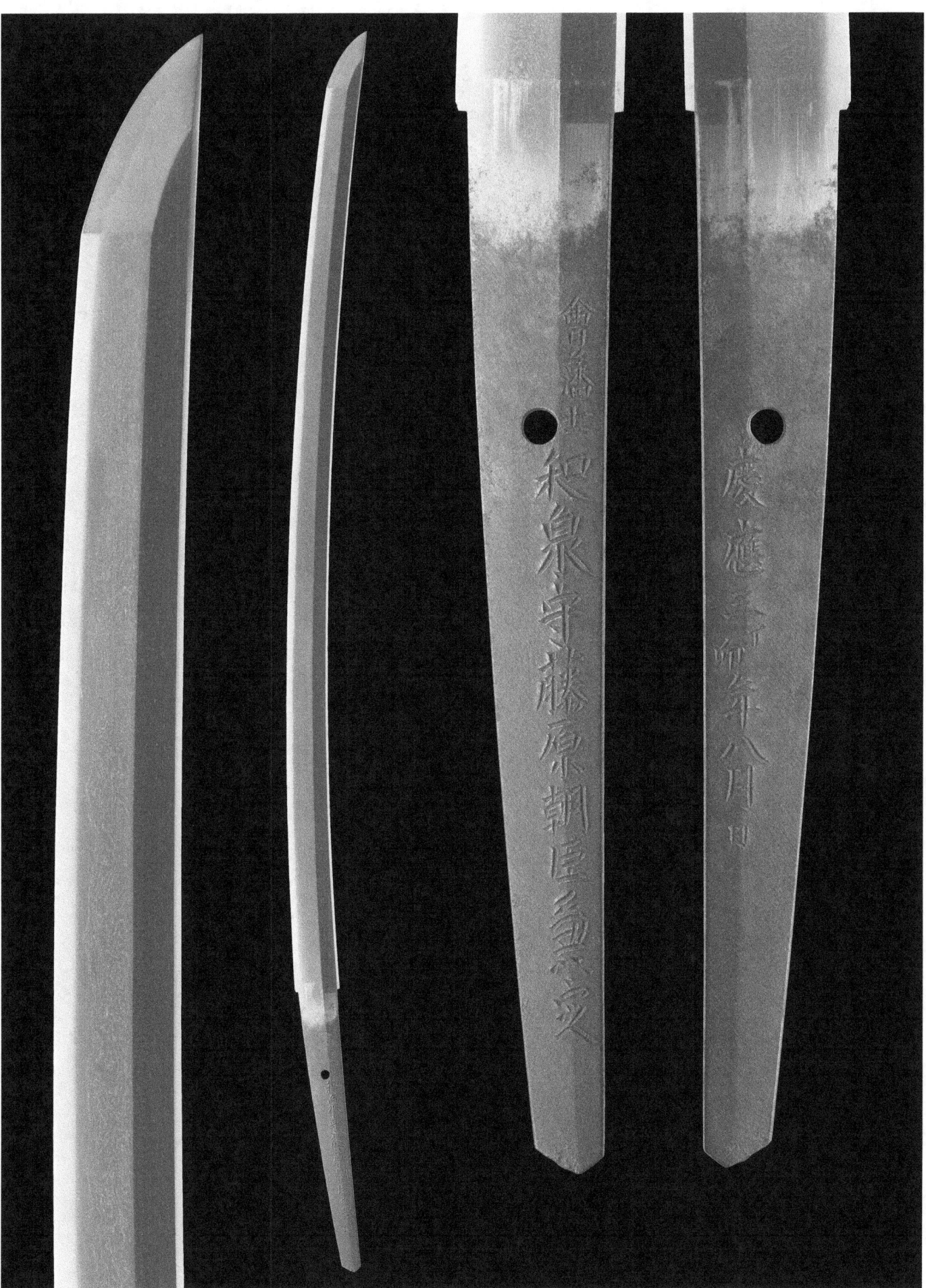

Katana

Mei:
Omote: *Izumi no Kami Fujiwara Ason Kanesada*
和泉守藤原朝臣兼定
Ura: *Keiō yon tsuchinoe-tatsu-doshi nigatsu hi*
慶應四戊辰年二月日
A day of the second month Keiō 4 [1868]
Nagasa: *2 shaku 3 sun 2 bu* (70,3 cm)
Sori: *5 bu* (1,5 cm)

Kanesada was 31 years old when he made this *Katana* in Keiō 4 (1868). The blade has a *Sugata* with a wide *Mihaba*, a relative wide *Shinogi-ji*, a high *Shinogi* and a *chō-Kissaki*, i.e. it looks quite sturdy.

The *Kitae* appears as very visible *Matsukawa-hada*, a forging structure which also belonged to the repertoire of Kanesada. And the *Hamon* is a carefully tempered *chū-Suguha* in *ko-Nie-deki* which is typical for Kanesada, accompanied by a *Sugu-bōshi* with a *Komaru-kaeri*. A high-quality blade which testifies to the great skill of the smith.

(Kawashima)

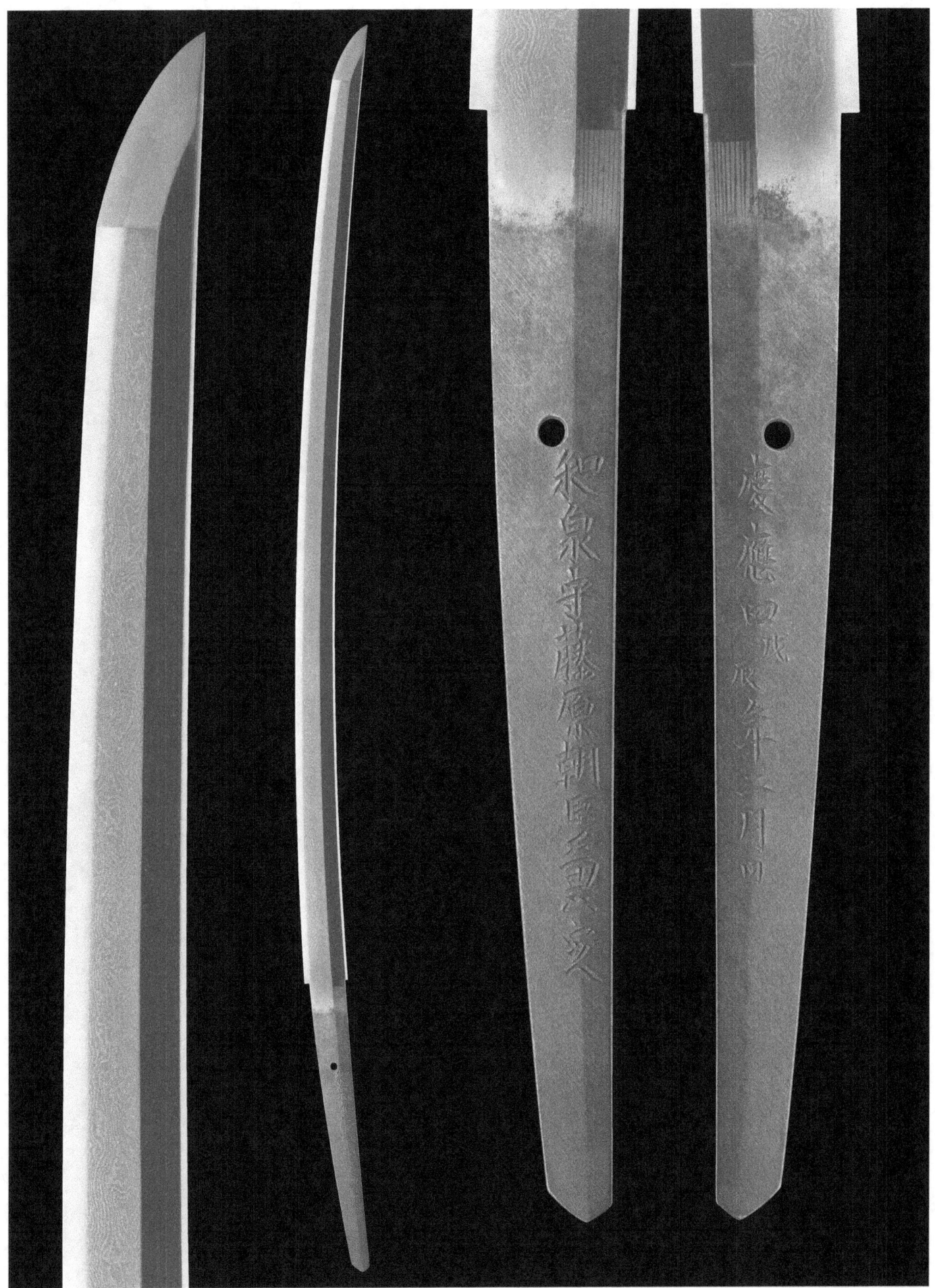

Tantō

Mei:
Omote: *Aizushi Izumi no Kami Kanesada*
　　　　會藩士　和泉守兼定
Ura:　*Keiō yo-nen hachi gatsu bi*
　　　　慶応四年八月日
　　　　A day of August, Keiō 4 [1868]
Nagasa: *8 sun* (24.2 cm)
Uchi-zori

This *Tantō* is *Hirazukuri*, almost *Muzori* and thicker *Kasane*. Strong *Nie* in *Habuchi* and *Jinie* followed by *Masame*. The *Hamon* became wider from *Monouchi* area towards to *Boshi* which intents to *Yamato-den Hosho* school. Keiō 4 (1868) is the year of Boshin war. In the same year the Aizu-han that Kanesada served was surrendered.

(Toyama)

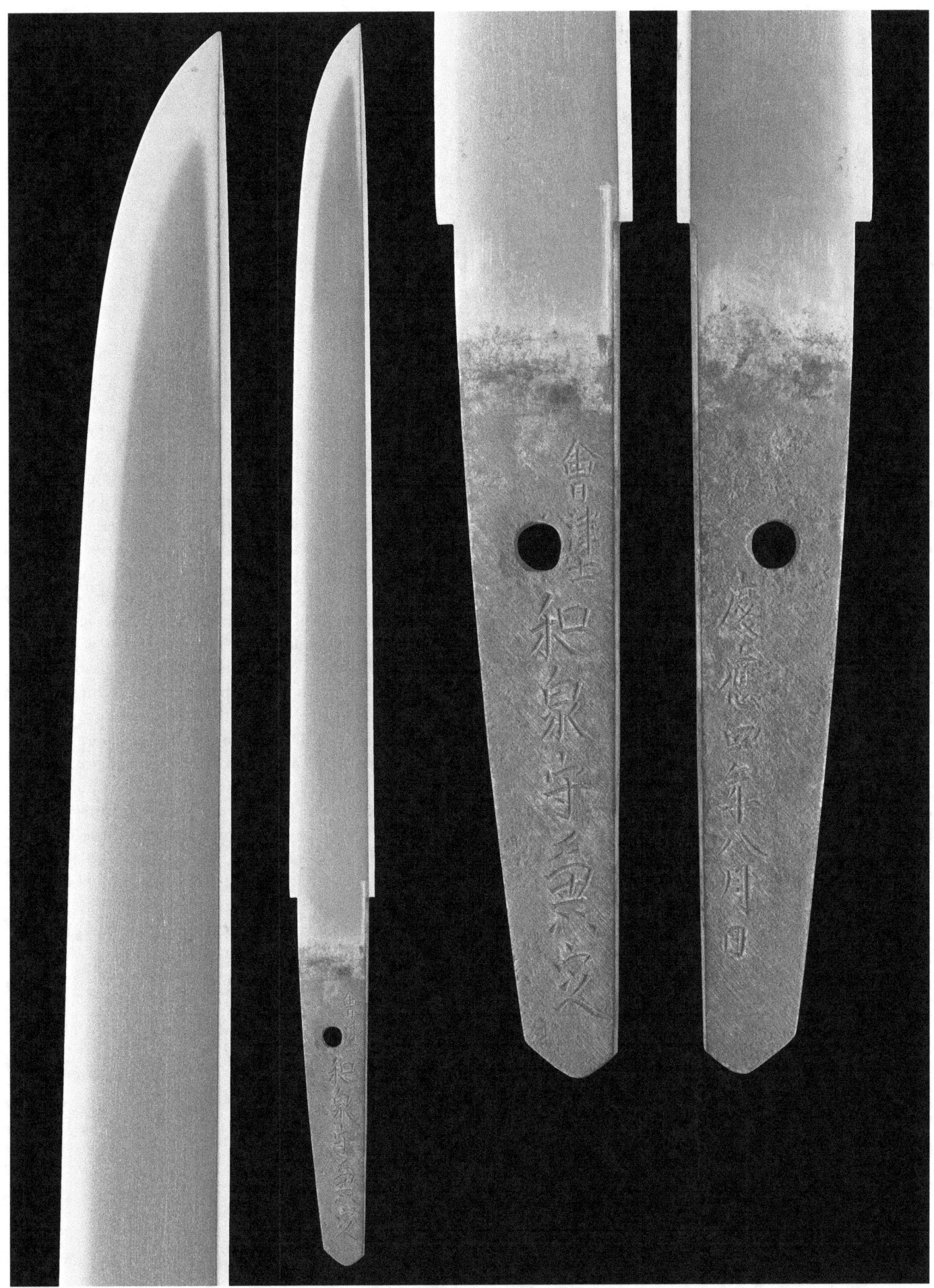

- 61 -

Wakizashi

Omote: Dai Nihon-kaji-sōshō – Izumi no
Kami Fujiwara Kanesada
大日本鍛冶宗匠・和泉守藤原兼定
Izumi no Kami Kanesada,
Master swordsmith of Japan
Ura: Keiō yon tsuchinoe-tatsu-doshi chūshū no hi
慶應四戊辰年仲秋日
A day in the middle of
Automn, Keiō 4 [1868]
Nagasa: 1 shaku 2 sun 6 bu (38,2 cm)
Sori: 2 bu 3 ri (0,7 cm)

Here we have a blade in *Unokubi-zukuri* with an *ō-Itame-hada* and *Masame* along the *Habuchi*. The *Hamon* is *Suguha* in *Nie-deki* with *Uchinoke*, *Kuichigaiba* and *Nijūba*. The *Bōshi* has a pointed and long *Kaeri* which runs back as *Muneyaki*. So from the point of view of *Sugata*, *Jigane* and *Hamon*, we have here an interpretation which is modelled on the Yamato tradition, or to be more precise, on the Shikkake school (尻懸) of the *Yamato-goha* (大和五派, "The Five Yamato Schools"). Also interesting is that the signature is – although undoubtedly executed by Kanesada himself – chiselled in a somewhat smaller and weaker manner than seen on other contemporary works.

The term *"Chūshū"* (仲秋) refers to the eighth lunar month. The battle for Aizu-Wakamatsu Castle started on the 23rd day of that month which lasted to the 22nd day of the following month when the castle surrendered. The previous *Tantō* is signed with "a day of the eighth month Keiō 4", but it has to be pointed out that it is very likely that this date does not refer to the actual production time as such dates like "a day of the eighth month" or "a day of the second month" were very often used by swordsmiths as a kind of auspicious dates. Apart from that, the signature of this *Tantō* is more powerfully chiselled than the one of this *Wakizashi*.

As mentioned, the supplement *Chūshū* narrows down the production time and is also the inscription "Dai Nihon-kaji-sōshō" (大日本鍛冶宗匠) is very rare. As for the supplement and the weakly chiselled *Mei*, it is possible that we are facing here a work from after the Aizu fief had surrendered, and that the defeat was very discouraging for Kanesada as having been a retainer of that fief his entire life. The honorary title "Nihon-kaji-sōshō" (日本鍛冶惣匠, later 日本鍛冶宗匠) was granted on a hereditary basis to the lineage of Iga no Kami Kinmichi (伊賀守金道). It was Tokugawa Ieyasu who granted it for the first time to the 1st generation Kinmichi and it was thereupon hardly in use outside of the Kinmichi line. According to the Meikan records, the Kinmichi line existed for ten generations and up to Kaei (嘉永, 1848-1854), but their whereabouts after that time are unclear. Well, it is unlikely that Kanesada used that title without anyone's permission and we can speculate that the Kanesada family allowed him to use it for whatever reason when they met when Kanesada was in Kyōto to receive via them his honorary title "Izumi no Kami." But this title does not appear on any earlier or later blade of Kanesada and so further studies are necessary to clarify this matter.

Incidentally, we occasionally find signatures of Kanesada in which he uses wrong characters. This one is such an example as he signed the character for *Ji* (治) in *Kaji* with the wrong character (治) (note the different left radical). Maybe in this case it is possible that he didn't have the habit of using and signing the honorary title in question, and made thus the mistake.

A very interesting and precious study piece of Kanesada with an excellent *Deki*.

(Kawashima)

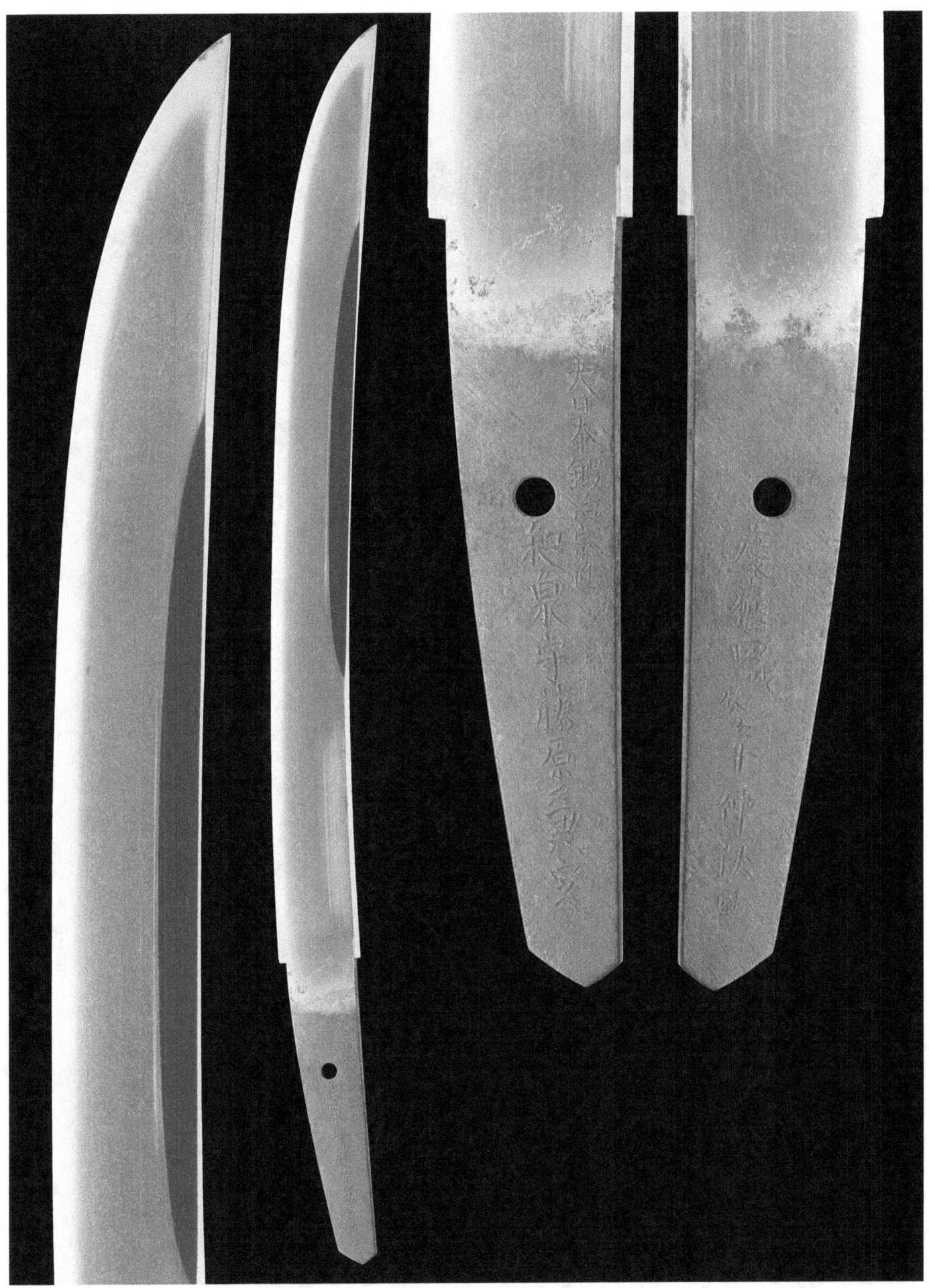

- 63 -

Katana

Mei:
Omote: *Iwashiro no Kuni-jū Izumi no Kami Kanesada*
岩代国住和泉守兼定
Izumi no Kami Kanesada,
resident of Iwashiro province
Ura: *Meiji ni hebidoshi hachigatsu hi*
明治二巳年八月日
A day of the eighth month
Meiji 2 [1869], year of the snake
Nagasa: *2 shaku 3 sun 1 bu* (70,0 cm)
Sori: *3 bu 3 ri* (1,0 cm)

This blade was made in Meiji 2 (1869), i.e. when Kanesada was 32 years old, the year he had to move in its ninth month to Kamo in Echigo province. It has a *Sugata* with a wide *Mihaba*, a thick *Moto-kasane* and *Saki-kasane*, and a high *Shinogi*, that means we are facing here quite a sturdy blade. The *Kitae* is an *Itame* mixed with *Mokume* and with a tendency to *Masame*. We can also see thick and peculiar *Chikei* which appear as standing-out areas of *ō-Mokume*. The *Hamon* is a form *chū-Suguha* in *ko-Nie-deki* which tends a bit to *Notare*. The *Nioiguchi* is wide and bright and many short *Ashi* can be seen and the *Bōshi* is lenient *Sugu-chō* with a *Komaru-kaeri*. An excellent blade of Kanesada.

(Kawashima)

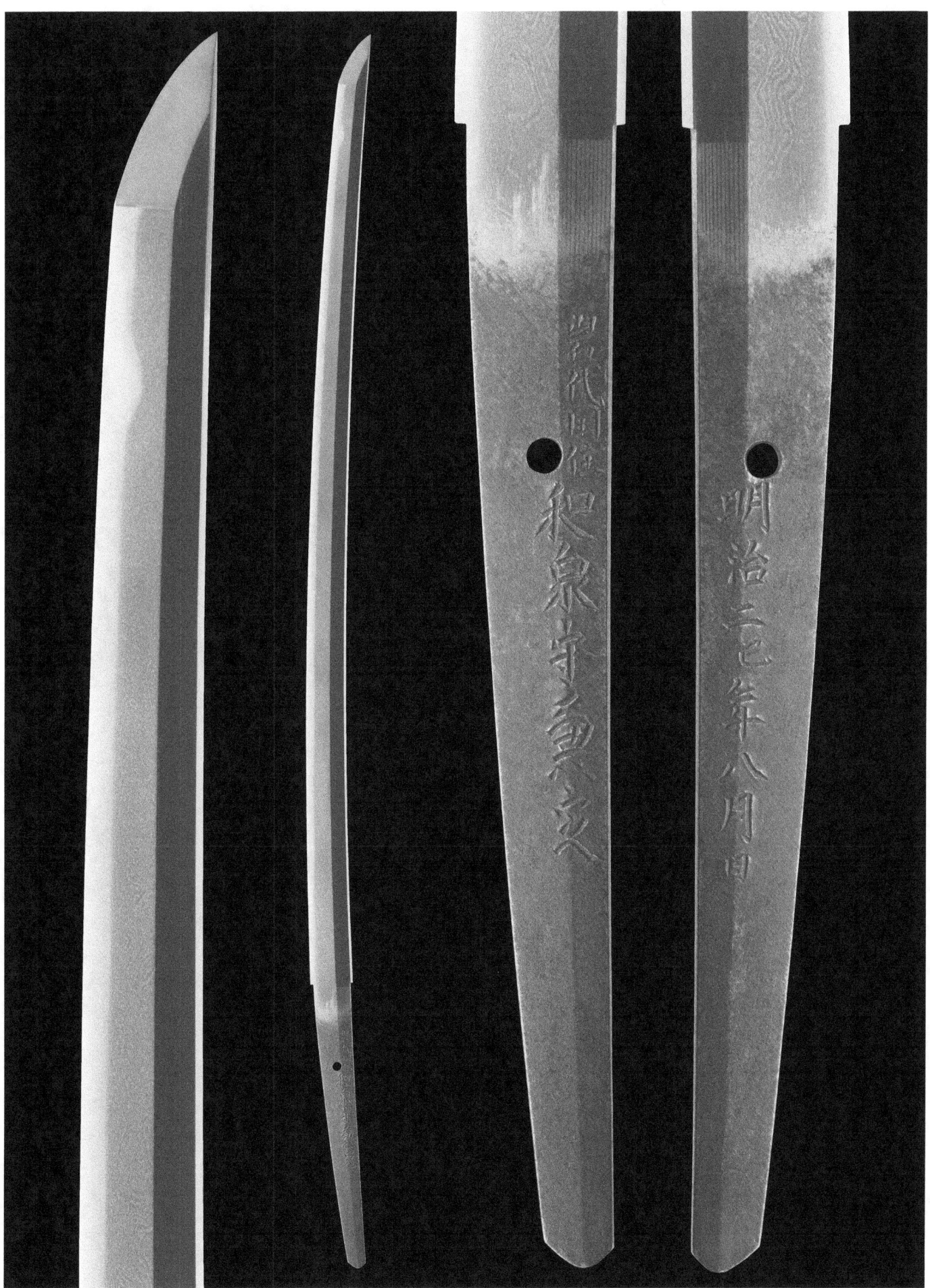

Tantō

Mei:
Omote: *Izumi no Kami Kanesada*
　　　　和泉守兼定
Ura:　　*Meiji ninen hachigatsu hi*
　　　　明治二年八月日
　　　　A day of the eighth month Meiji 2 [1869]
Nagasa: 7 sun 4 bu (22,4 cm)
Uchizori

The blade is in *Kanmuri-otoshi* with *Moroha* and a thick *Yoroidōshi*-style *Kasane*. Many *Kotō* era *Kanmuri-otoshi Tantō* go back to smiths of Yamato smiths and this blade was also interpreted by Kanesada in the Yamato tradition. That means it shows a well and densely forged *Masame* and a varied *Suguha*-based *Hamon* in ko-*Nie-deki* with *Kuichigaiba*, *Hotsure* and *Uchinoke* and a uniform *Gunome* with roundish *Yakigashira* as *Kaeri* along the *Moroha* cutting edge. The *Ura* side of the *Nakago* is dated Meiji 1 (1869).

(Kawashima)

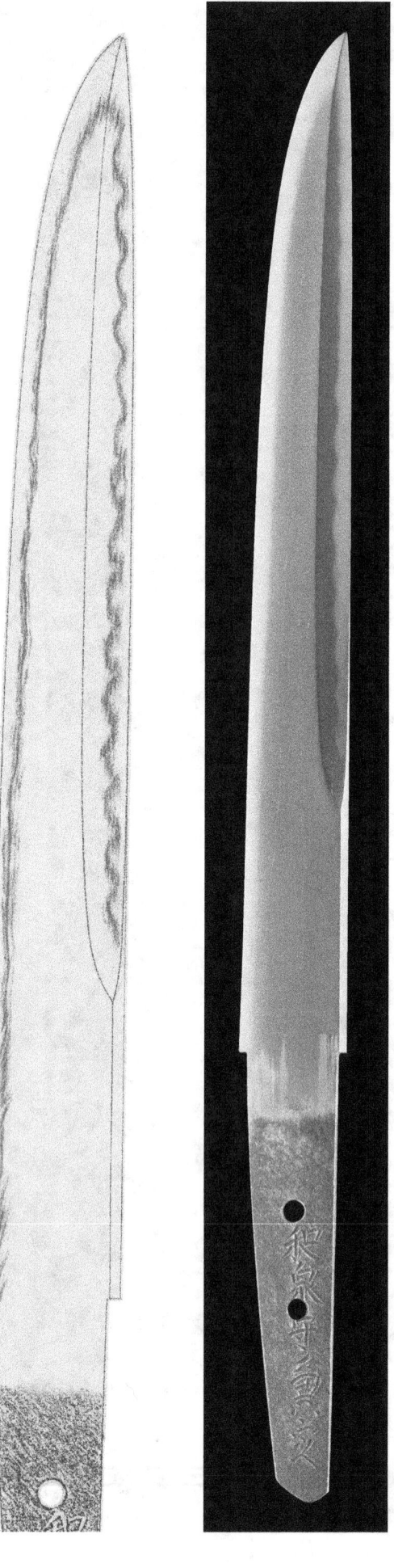

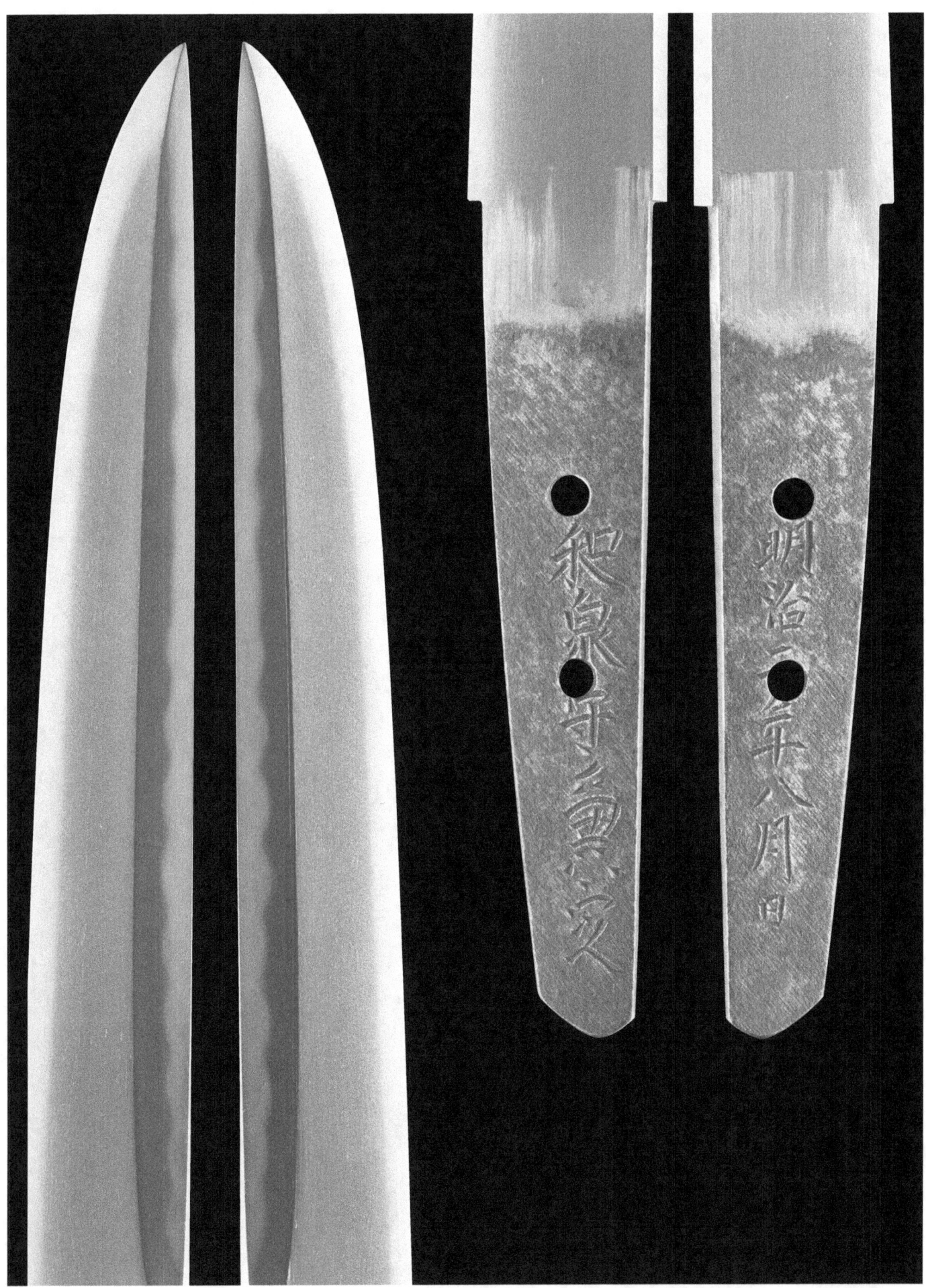

Katana

Mei:
Omote: Iwashiro no Kuni-jū Kanesada
　　　　岩代國住兼定
Ura:　Meiji sannen nigatsu hi
　　　　明治三年二月日
　　　　A day of the second month Meiji 3 [1870]
Nagasa: 2 shaku 2 sun 5 bu (68,2 cm)
Sori:　4 bu (1,3 cm)

The blade has the Kanesada-typical "standard length" and a very harmonious and matching *Sori*. The *Kissaki* in turn is a somewhat elongated *chū-Kissaki*, the *Shinogi-ji* is wide and the *Shinogi* is high. The *Kitae* is a very dense *Masame* with plentiful of *Ji-nie* and the *Hamon* a *chū-Suguha* in *ko-Nie-deki* with a wide, uniform, bright and clear *Nioiguchi*. The *Bōshi* appears as *chū-Suguha* with a *Komaru-kaeri*, is quite *Ko-nie*-loaden and shows *Hakikake*. Partially some *Kuichigaiba* and *Uchinoke* appears what speaks for Yamato tradition *Hataraki*. So we are facing here a textbook *Masame* and Yamato-inspired interpretation of Kanesada, which is typical for that time. Apart from that, the *Deki* is excellent.

The supplement "Iwakuni-jū" appears on his blades from the second year of Meiji onwards. The Aizu fief had surrendered to the new Meiji government in the ninth month of Keiō 4 (= Meiji 1, 1868) and the lands fell into imperial possession. That means we can assume that this was the reason why Kanesada no longer signed with supplements like "Aihan-shi" or "Aiyō-shin" – i.e. "retainer of the Aizu fief" – and switched to the neutral "Iwashiro no Kuni-jū" ("resident of Iwashiro province"). So looking at the changes in Kanesada´s signatures we can get a vivid picture of the turbulent times back then.

(Kawashima)

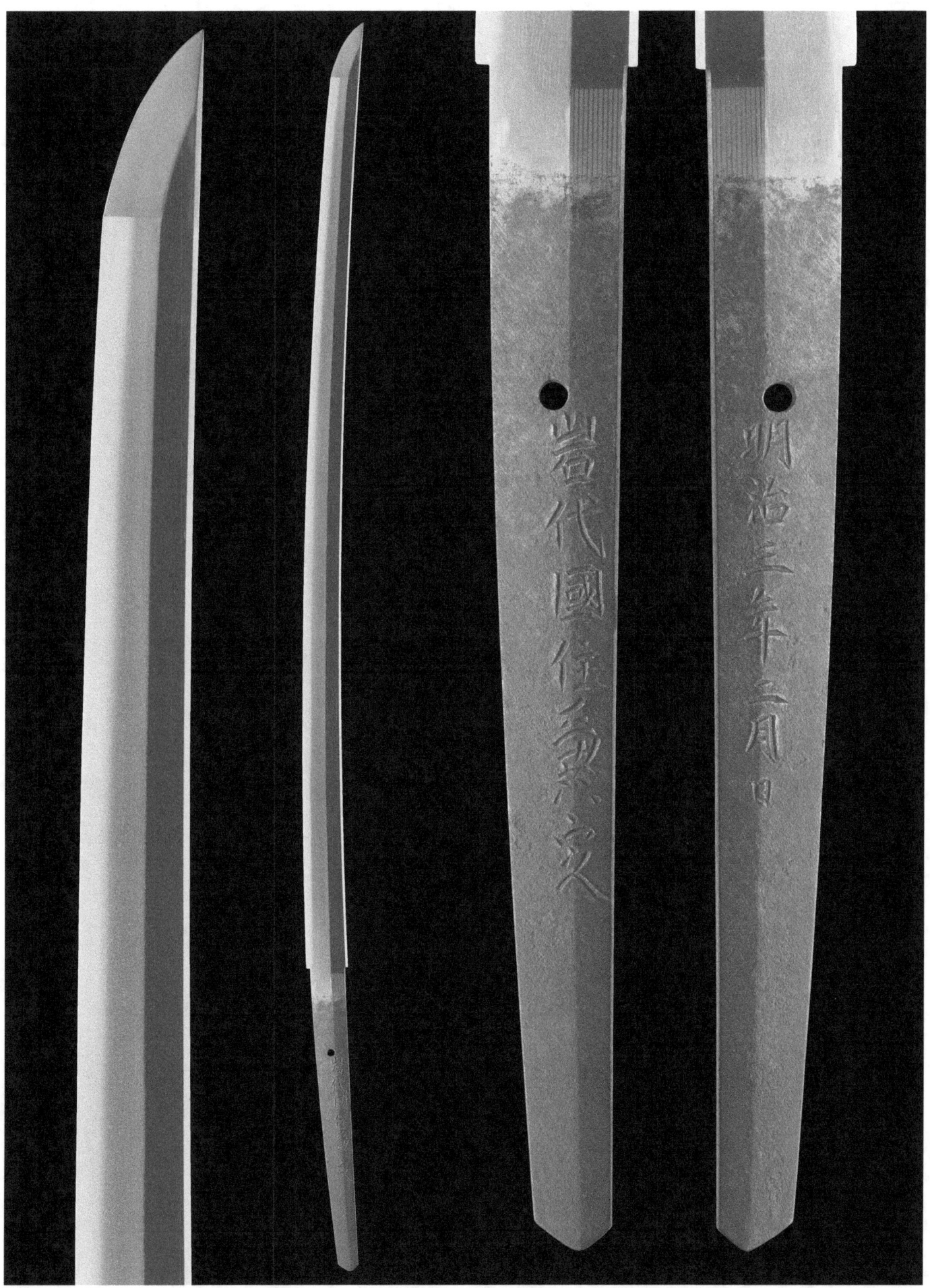

Katana

Mei:
Omote: Iwashiro no Kuni Iyumi no Kami Kanesada
　　　　岩代國和泉守兼定
Ura:　Meiji sannen hachigatsu hi –
　　　　Kotō iri shihozume o motte tsukuru –
　　　　Shikōshite Inoue Kanezane no tame
　　　　明治三年八月日・以古刀鑄四
　　　　方詰造・而為井上務實
　　　　A day of the eighth month Meiji 3 [1870],
　　　　forged in the *Shihōzume* technique by
　　　　using processed steel from a *Kotō* blade
Nagasa: 2 *shaku* 1 *sun* (63,6 cm)
Sori:　 3 *bu* 3 *ri* (1,0 cm)

Kanesada's blades are hardly interpreted in the exaggerated and magnificent *Sugata* so popular during *Shinshintō* times. They settle around 70 cm and are very well balanced in terms of proportions and handling. Although this blade has just a little *Sori*, it does not look too straight, and this shallow curvature is a factor for the result we see, namely a blade with a harmonious *Sugata*. The *Jigane* shows *Ji-nie* and strong *Chikei*, a feature which is also typical for Kanesada, and tends with the *Mokume-nagare* as so-called *Ayasugi-hada*. The *Hamon* is a *chū-Suguha* in *ko-Nie-deki* with relative distinct *Hataraki* like *Ashi* and *Yō*. The *Nakago* is rather long compared to the *Nagasa* and is signed firmly with a thick chisel. Very interesting is the additional information of the commissioner and that the blade was forged from processed steel from a *Kotō* blade and in the *Shihōzume* technique. However, details on Inoue Kanezane (the characters of his first name can also read "Chikazane", "Michizane" or "Nakazane") are unclear but the blade has the typical excellent *Deki* for a *Chūmon-uchi*.

(Kawashima)

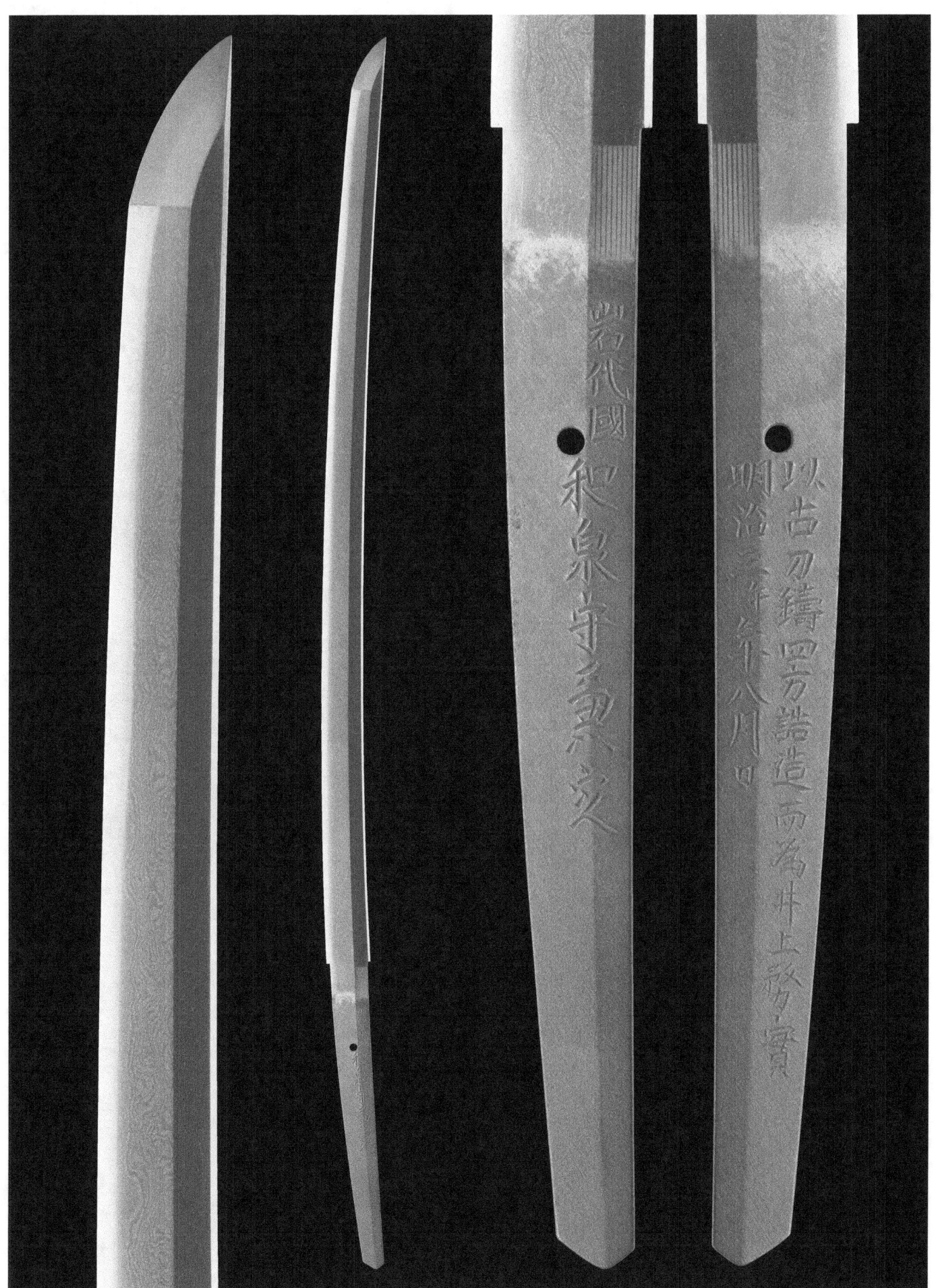

Tantō

Mei:
Omote: Izumi No Kami Kanesada
和泉守兼定
Ura: Meiji sannen hachi gatsu bi
和泉守兼定
A day of August, Meiji 3 [1870]
Nagasa: 8 sun 8 bu (26.7 cm)
Muzori

Sugata is thick *Kasane Unokubi-zukuri*. *Jitestsu* is very fine uniformed *Masame*. *Hamon* is *Suguha* tight *Nioguchi* with strong *Nie* and *Kinsunji*. This blade is serene steel with strong tempering made *Nie* stronger than average.

(Toyama)

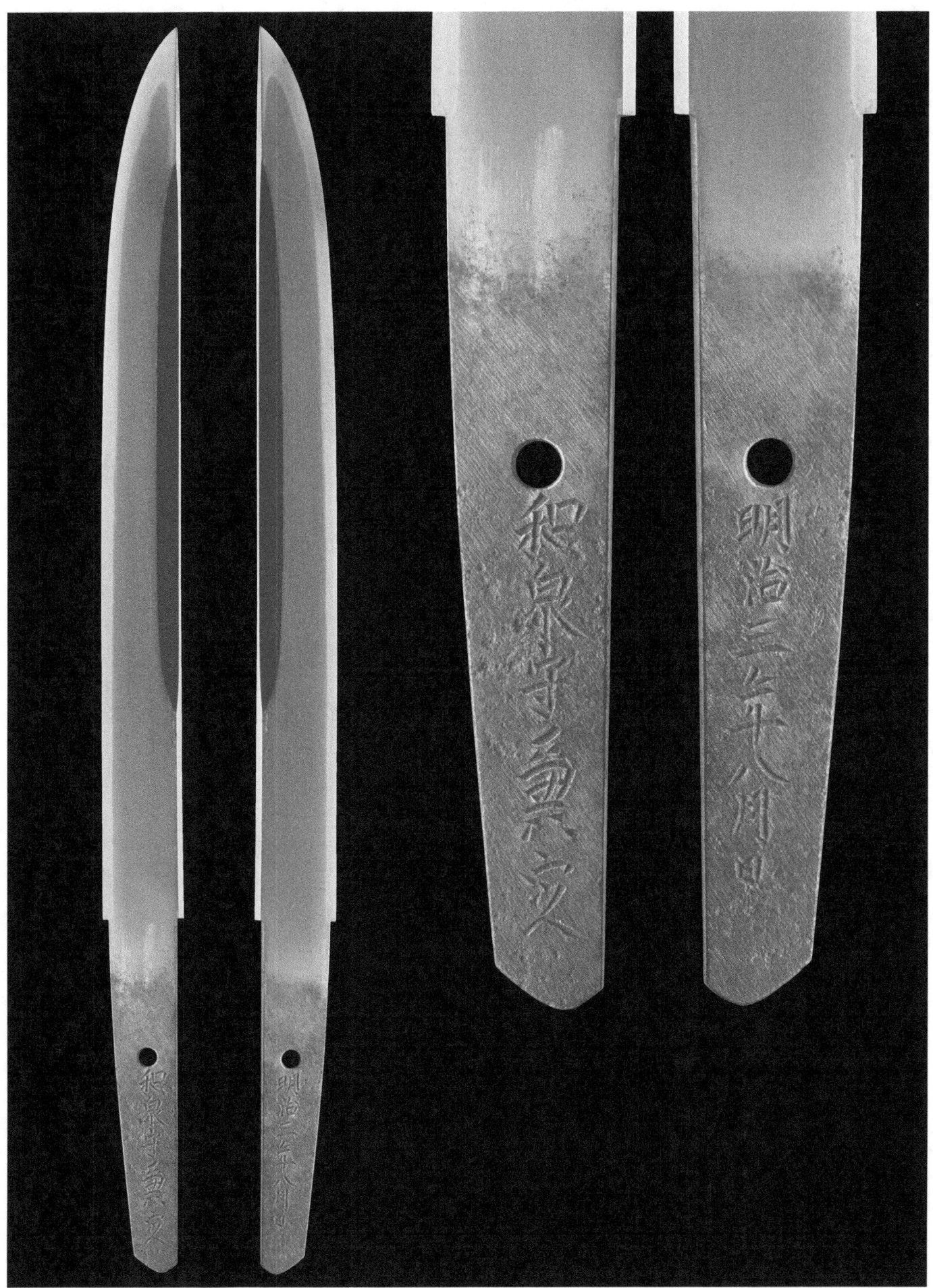

Ken

Mei:
Omote: Suwa Daijin
諏訪太神
The god of Suwa Jinja shrine
Ura: Hono Meji yonen hitsuji san gatsu bi machi (no) Anzen (no) tame Kamo (ni) oite Kanesada
奉納　明治四年未三月日
為町安全　於賀茂　兼定
Dedication for the safety of the town at Kamo, a day of March, Meiji 4 [1871], the year of the sheep
Nagasa: 8 sun 1 bu (24.5 cm)
Muzori

Jitetsu is *Mokume* with fine *Shirake Utsuri*, *Hadadatsu*. It is not *Masame* but is very stretched *Mokume*. *Hamon* is *Futo (Hiro)-suguha* with small *Midare*. The wide *Mihaba Ken* with *Futo-suguha* as well as the *Jitetsu* being very stretched *Mokume*, almost *Masame* is very rare for his work. There is Kanesada's sword donated to the Suwa Jinja Shrine in Shibata City, but there is another Suwa Jinja Shrine in Kamo. Therefore it is not sure which Suwa Jinja it is made for. This sword is made for the donation. That is why whole cutting edge is *Ububa*. It has been never sharpened. It is written: "Kichō shirio no ichi (one of the important evidence, Sayagaki by Satō Kanzan).

(Toyama)

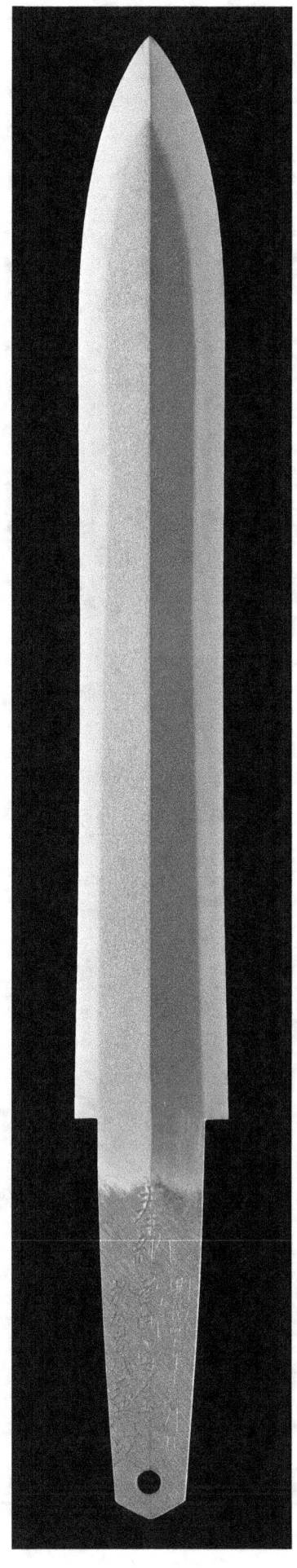

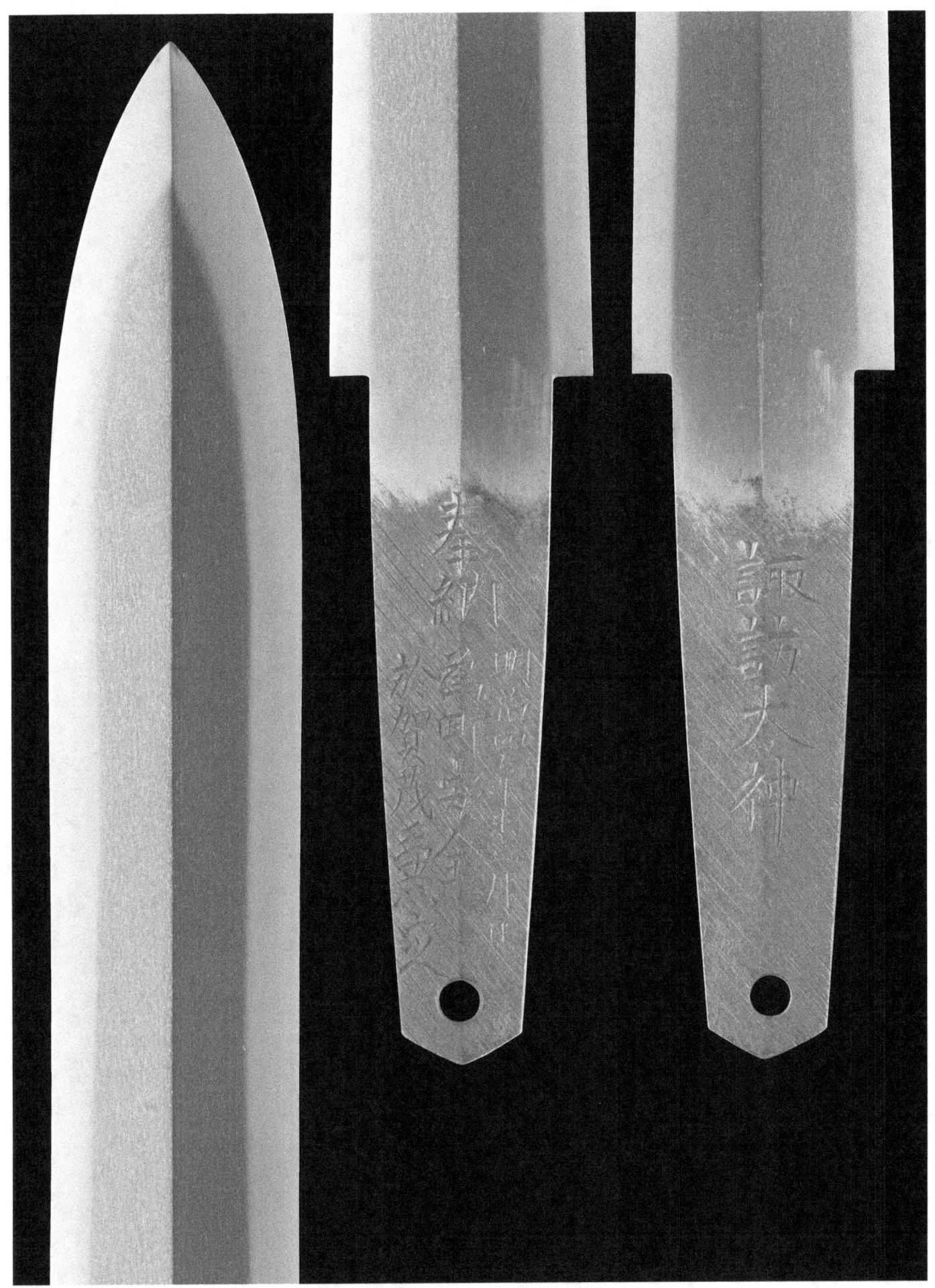

Tantō

Mei:
Omote: Izumi no Kami Kanesada
和泉守兼定
Ura: Meiji yon kanoto-hitsuji-doshi haru (no) hi
明治四辛未年春日
A day of Spring, Meiji 4 [1871]
Nagasa: 9 sun (27.3 cm)
Muzori

Jitetsu is tight *kō-Mokume* with *Nagare Hada* in the bottom. *Hamon* is based on *Suguha* and mellow *Notare* with *kō-Nie* in *Habuchi*. There *Kuichigaiba* below *Monouchi* on both *Omote* and *Ura* side. It is a little bit thicker *Kasane* but of a slim and elegant shape.

(Toyama)

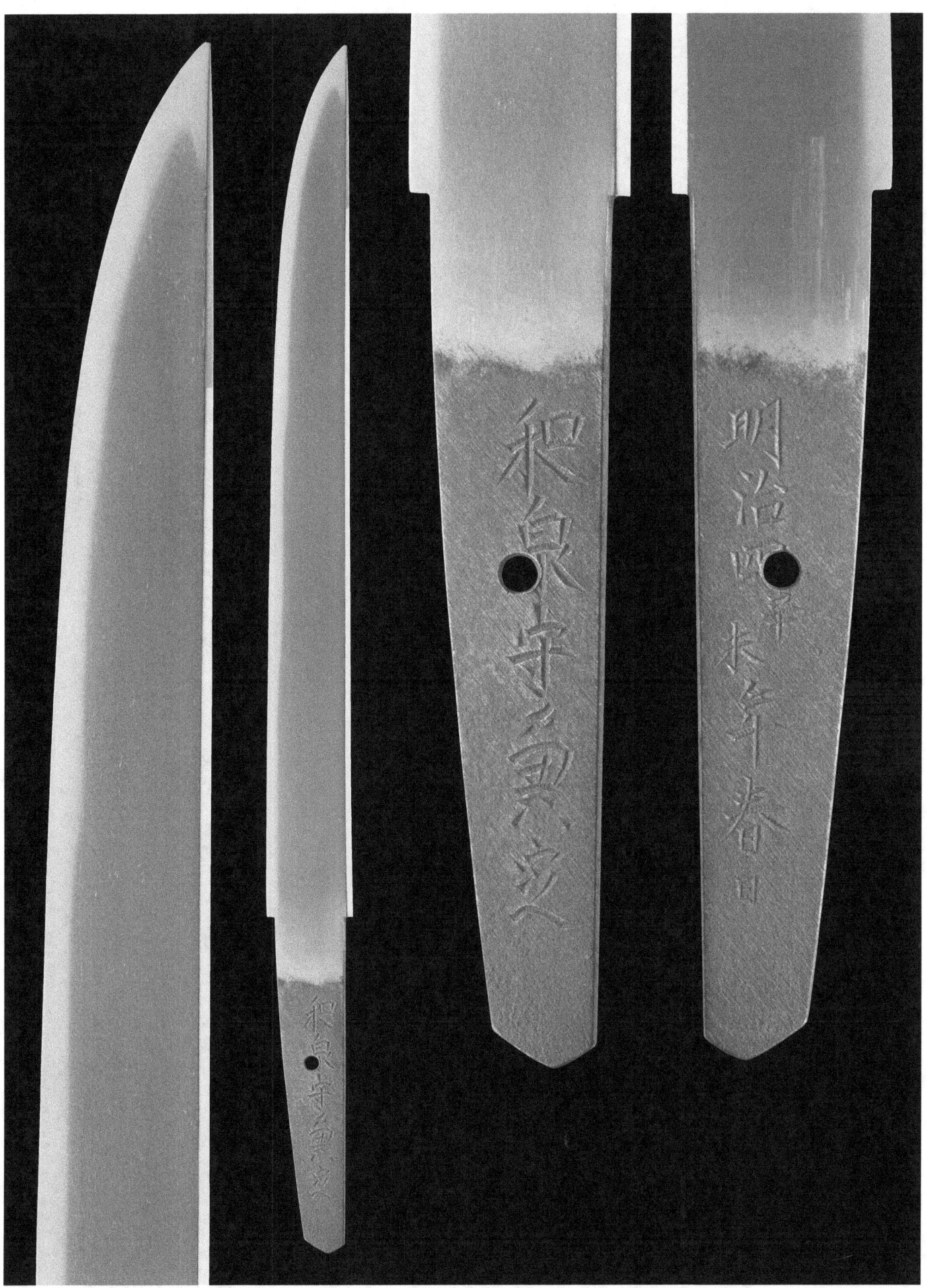

- 77 -

Tantō

Mei:
Omote: *Asahimaru Izumi no Kami Kanesada*
旭丸　和泉守兼定
Ura: *Meiji yon kanoto-hitsuji-doshi go-gatsu jūyokka Namufukashigikō Nyoray*
明治辛未年五月十四日　南無不可思議光如来
14th of May, Meiji 4 [1871], Namufukashigikō Nyoray (Amitābha)
Mune: *Etsu Kamijō Higashi (...) Nobunari (no) motome ōgon (wo) kuae kore (wo) tsukuru*
越上条東□延成需加黄金造之
Ordered by Higashi (...) Nobunari and forged with added gold at Kamijō in Hokuetsu
Nagasa: 8 sun 8 Bu kyo (26.7+ cm)
Muzori

It is a longish *Tantō*. *Jitetsu* is tight *kō-Mokume* with bright fine *Jinie*. *Hamon* is based on big and small *Gunome* and *Notare* with *Nie* in *Habuchi*, many activity in deep *Nioiguchi*. Both *Ji* and *Ha* are very bright and clear. It is very well done. The signature above *Mekugiana* on *Omote* "Asahimaru" is the name of this *Tantō*. It is very rare for Kanesada to cut in this way.

"Namufukashigikō Nyoray" on *Ura* is the other calling name of "Amitābha", as "Kuji-miogo" for "Jōdoshinshū" (one of the Buddism school). That is why we think the person who had ordered this *Tantō* was a believer of this school. The signature "Etsu" on *Mune* means Hokuetsu, "Kamijō" is the Kamijō village next to Kamo village. This village is integrated into Kamo city today. Other signature "ōgon (wo) kuae kore (wo) tsukuru" means that gold was added while forging. We find same signature in the sword made by Taikei Naotane in Shinshintō period but not in any other work of Kanesada. We can imagine the person who ordered this *Tantō* heard about the sword with gold made by Taikei Naotane and specially ordered it to Kanesada. Those special signatures on this *Tantō* is a very rare work and this is the only example existing.

(Toyama)

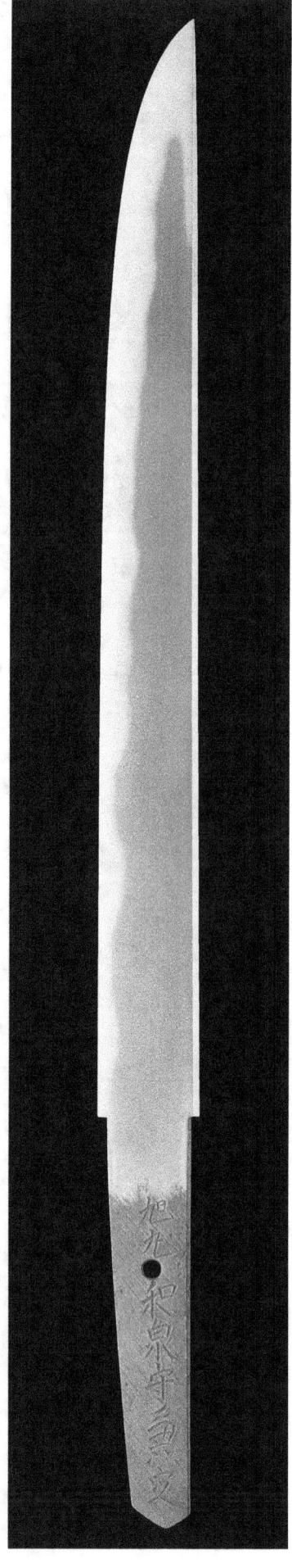

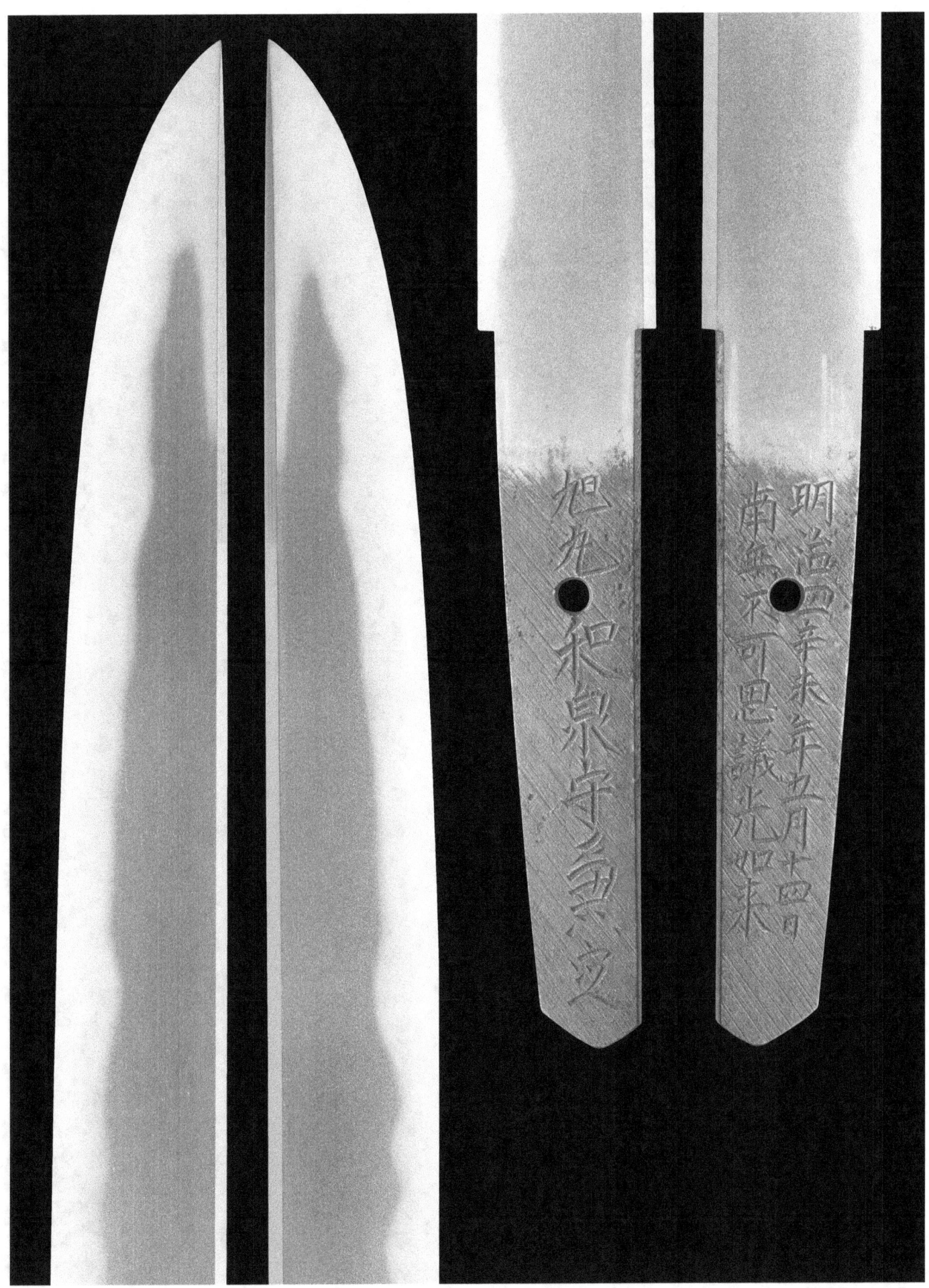

Tantō

Mei:
Omote: *Kamo ni oite – Izumi no Kami Kanesada*
於加茂・和泉守兼定
Ura: *Sanbyakunen-mae tsukutta kotō*
o motte kore o agegitae
以三[百]年前古刀製上鍛之
Carefully forged from a 300 years old Kotō
Mune: *Meiji yon kanoto-hitsujidoshi hachigatsu hi*
明治辛未年八月日
A day of the eighth month Meiji 4 [1871]
Nagasa: 5 *sun* 6 *bu* (17,3 cm)
Muzori

From the inscription of the tang we learn that this *Tantō* was made in Meiji 4 (1871) in Kamo in Echigo province. It is in *Hira-zukuri*, has an *Uchizori*, thick *Kasane*, *Futasuji-hi* on the *Omote*, and a *Bōhi* on the *Ura* side which runs with *Kaki-nagashi*. The *Kitae* is a ko-*Itame* mixed with *Masame* shows plentiful of *Ji-nie*. The *Hamon* is a *Suguha-chō* mixed with shallow *Notare*, *Ashi* and *Kinsuji*. The inscription that Kanesada made this *Tantō* from a 300 years old *Kotō* makes this blade quite a rarity but apart from that also an important reference.

(Kawashima)

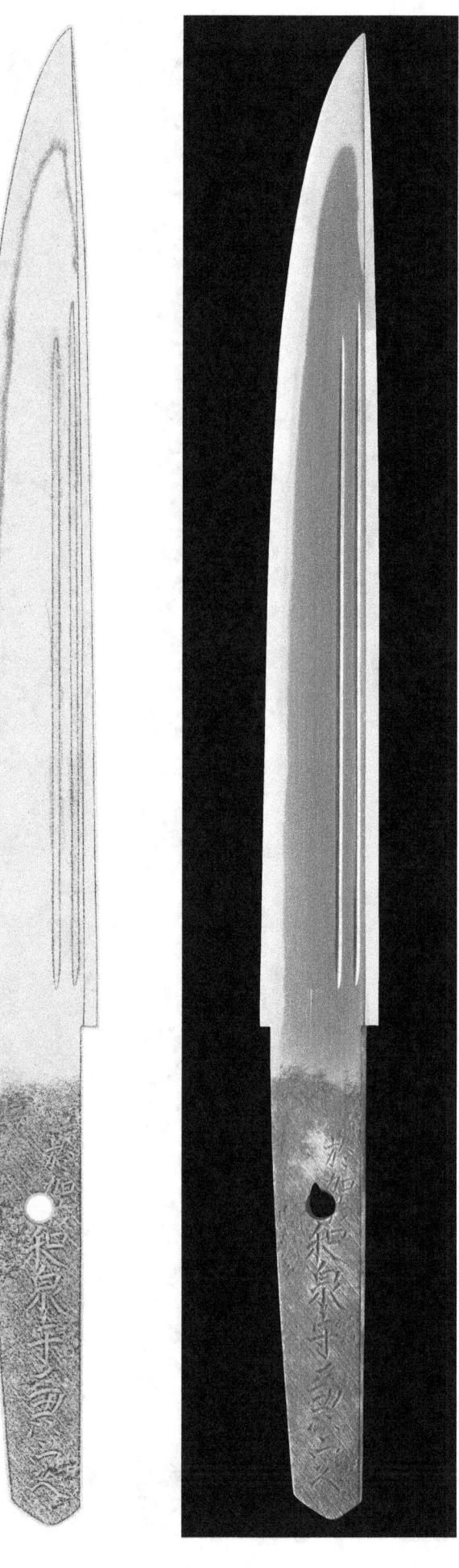

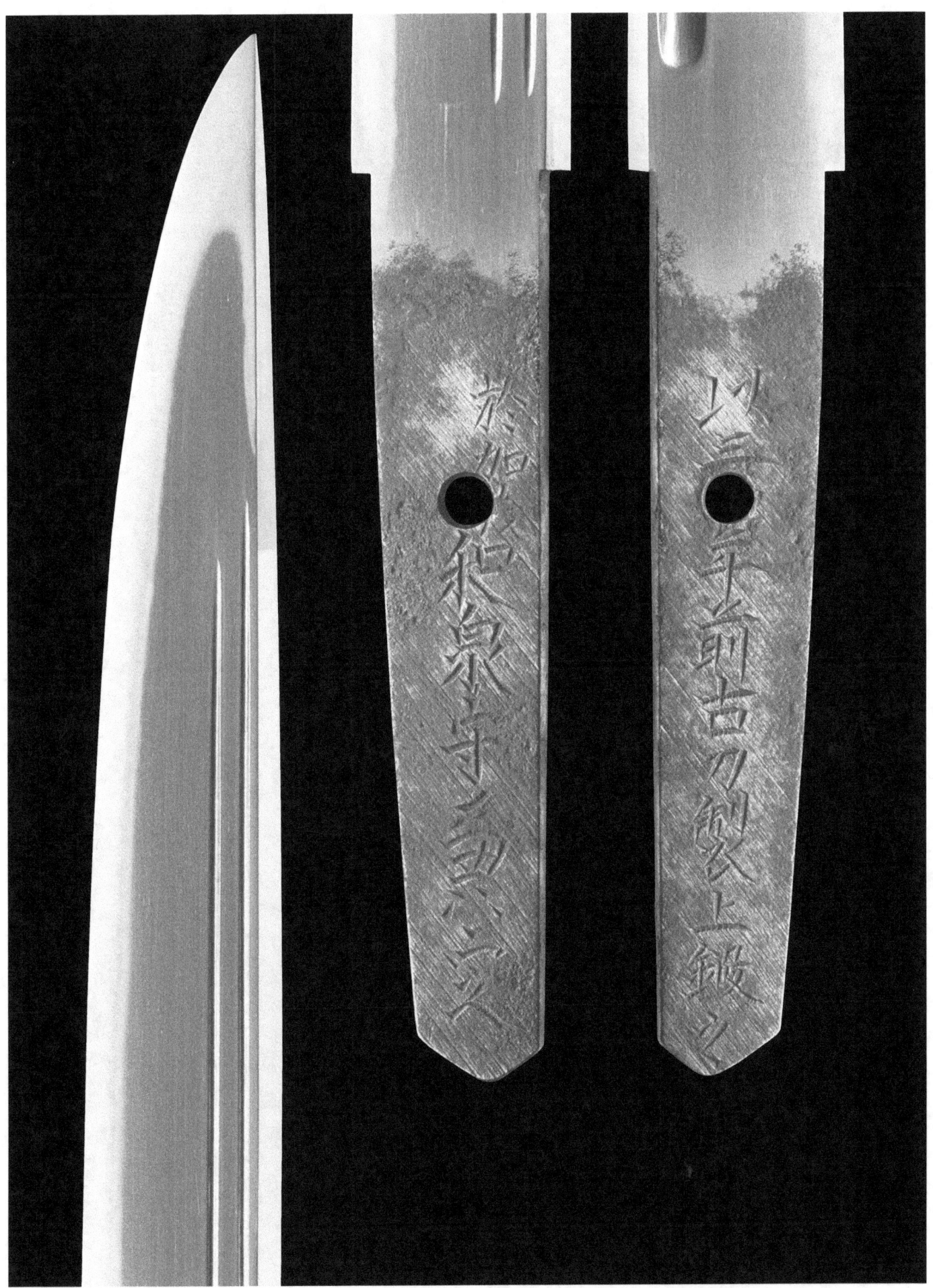

Wakizashi

Mei:
Omote: *Izumi no Kami Kanesada*
和泉守兼定
Ura: *Meiji rokunen hachigatsu hi*
明治六年八月日
A day of the eighth month Meiji 6 [1873]
Nagasa: 1 *shaku* 3 *sun* 1 *bu* (39,7 cm)
Sori: 1 *bu* 6 *ri* (0,5 cm)

Kanesada was 37 years old in Meiji 6 (1873). This blade is in *Shinogi-zukuri* and has a normal *Sugata* but with the typically high *Shinogi* for Kanesada. The *Jigane* is *Itame* mixed with *Mokume* with *Jinie*, the *Hamon* is *Sanbonsugi*-like *Gunome* in *ko-Nie-deki*, and the *Bōshi* up to about the middle of the *Kissaki* is *Midare-komi*. The *Mei* is done with a fine chisel and in a fluent manner what is often seen on blades made in Kamo. This *Wakizashi* is dated Meji 6, therefore this is also a sword made in Kamo.

(Kawashima)

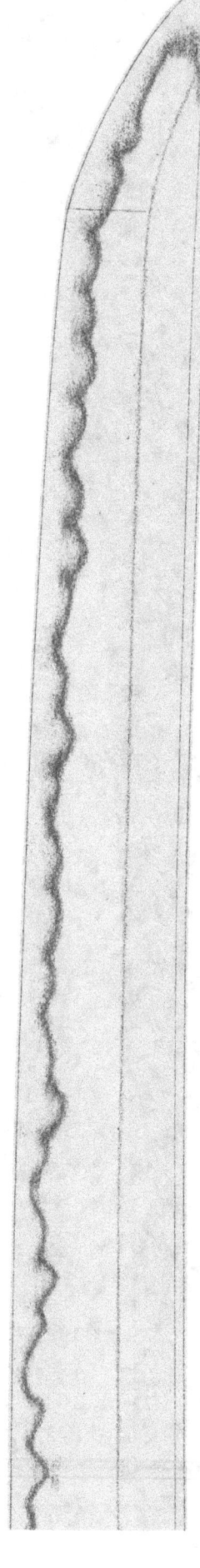

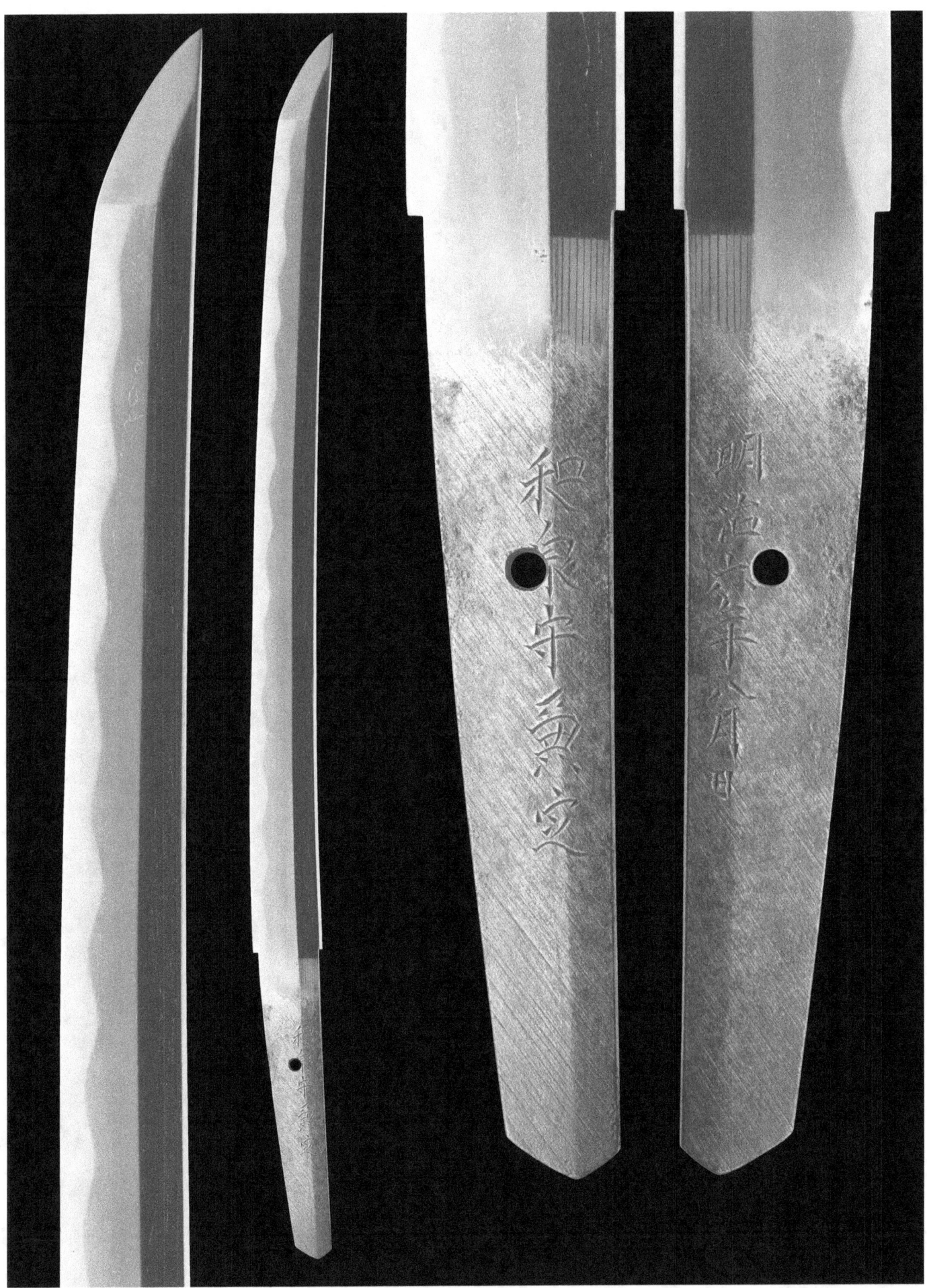

Tantō

Mei:
Omote: Dai Nihon Kamo Kanesada
　　　　大日本加茂兼定
Ura: 　Kigen nisengohyakusanjūyonen nigatsu
　　　　紀元二千五百三十四年二月
　　　　Second month of the 2,534th anniversary of the imperial era
Nagasa: 6 sun 5 bu (19,7 cm)
Uchizori

This blade is in *Hira-zukuri* and shows a little *Uchizori* which results in this case in a so-called *Takenoko-zori*. And with the thick *Kasane*, we have here a *Tantō* in *Yoroidōshi* manner. The *Kitae* is a very dense *ko-Itame* which is partially mixed with some *Masame*. The *Hamon* is quite a tight *chū-Suguha* in *ko-Nie-deki* and the *Bōshi* is *Komaru* and long *Kaeri*.

　The date on the *Ura* side of the tang counts the years since the inthronisation of Japan's Emperor Jinmu and corresponds to Meiji 7 (1874). Such a signature which refers to the anniversary of the imperial era is called *Kōki-nenki* (皇紀銘) and this *Tantō* is one of the earliest known blades bearing such a *Kōki-nenki*. The suffix "Dai Nihon" appears frequently on Kanesada's works from Keiō 4 (慶応, 1868) onwards but the combination "Dai Nihon Kamo" is rare. Maybe this is the one and the only blade of Kanesada signed that way.

(Kawashima)

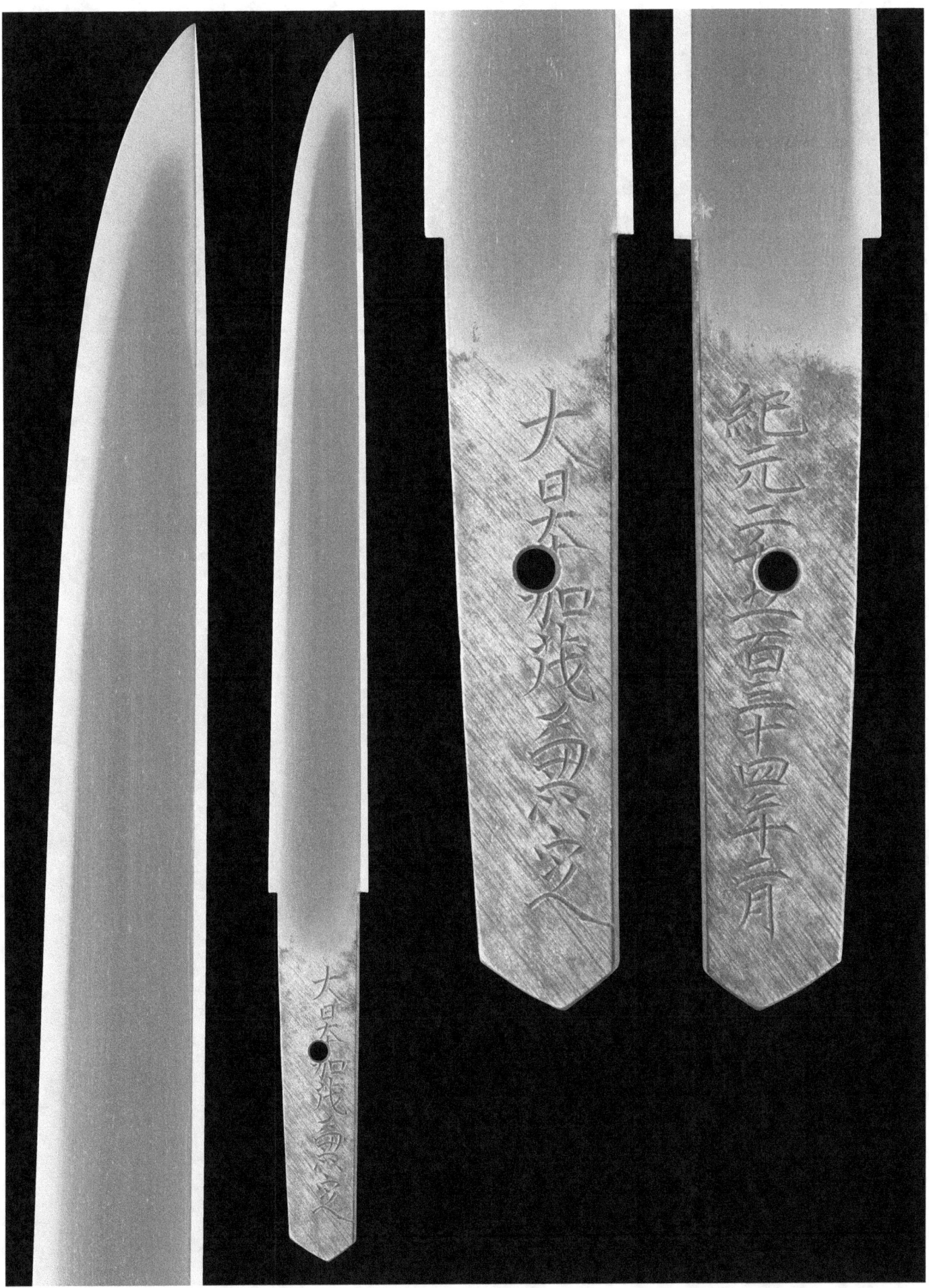

Tantō

Mei:
Omote: *Izumi no Kami Kanesada*
和泉守兼定
Ura: *Echigo no Kuni ni oite tsukuru*
於越後国造
Made in Echigo province
Nagasa: 9 *sun* 3 *bu* 1 *ri* (28,2 cm)
Sori: 1 *bu* (0,3 cm)

This blade is in *Hira-zukuri* with just a little *Sori*. The *Jigane* is a very dense *ko-Itame* with plentiful of *Ji-nie*. The *Hamon* is tight *Suguha* in *ko-Nie-deki* with a quite tight *Nioiguchi* which is mixed with some *Ashi* and *Yō* and a little *Gunome* from the *Monouchi* area towards the tip. The *Ura* side's signature "Echigo no Kuni ni oite tsukuru" is rare.

(Kawashima)

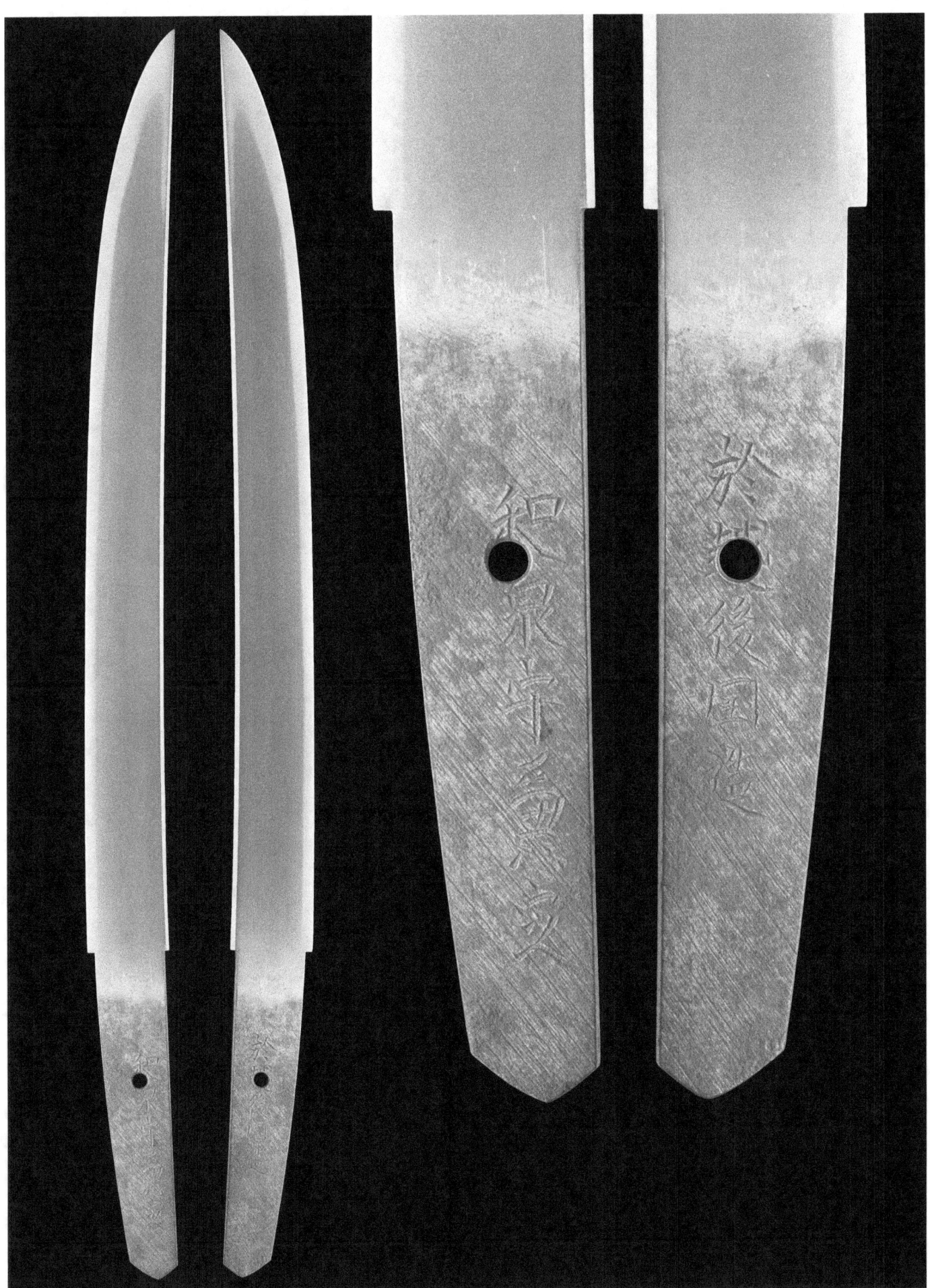

Tantō

Mei:
Omote: Izumi no Kami Kanesada
         和泉守兼定
Ura: Usami Sukeyoshi (no) motome (ni) ōzu
         Echigo no kuni Kamo (ni) oite tsukuru
         鷹宇佐美裕愛需　於越後国賀茂造
         Accepted order from Usami Sukeyoshi,
         made at Kamo in Echigo province
Nagasa: 7 sun 4 bu (22.4 cm)
Muzori

Jitetsu is very tight *ko-Mokume* with fine *Jinie*. *Hamon* is *Suguha*. This is very rare Yamashiro-den *Tantō* made by Kanesada. It looks like Kotō Awataguchi blade, very fine tight *Kitae* is almost transparent. The orderer Usami Sukeyoshi is unknown.

(Toyama)

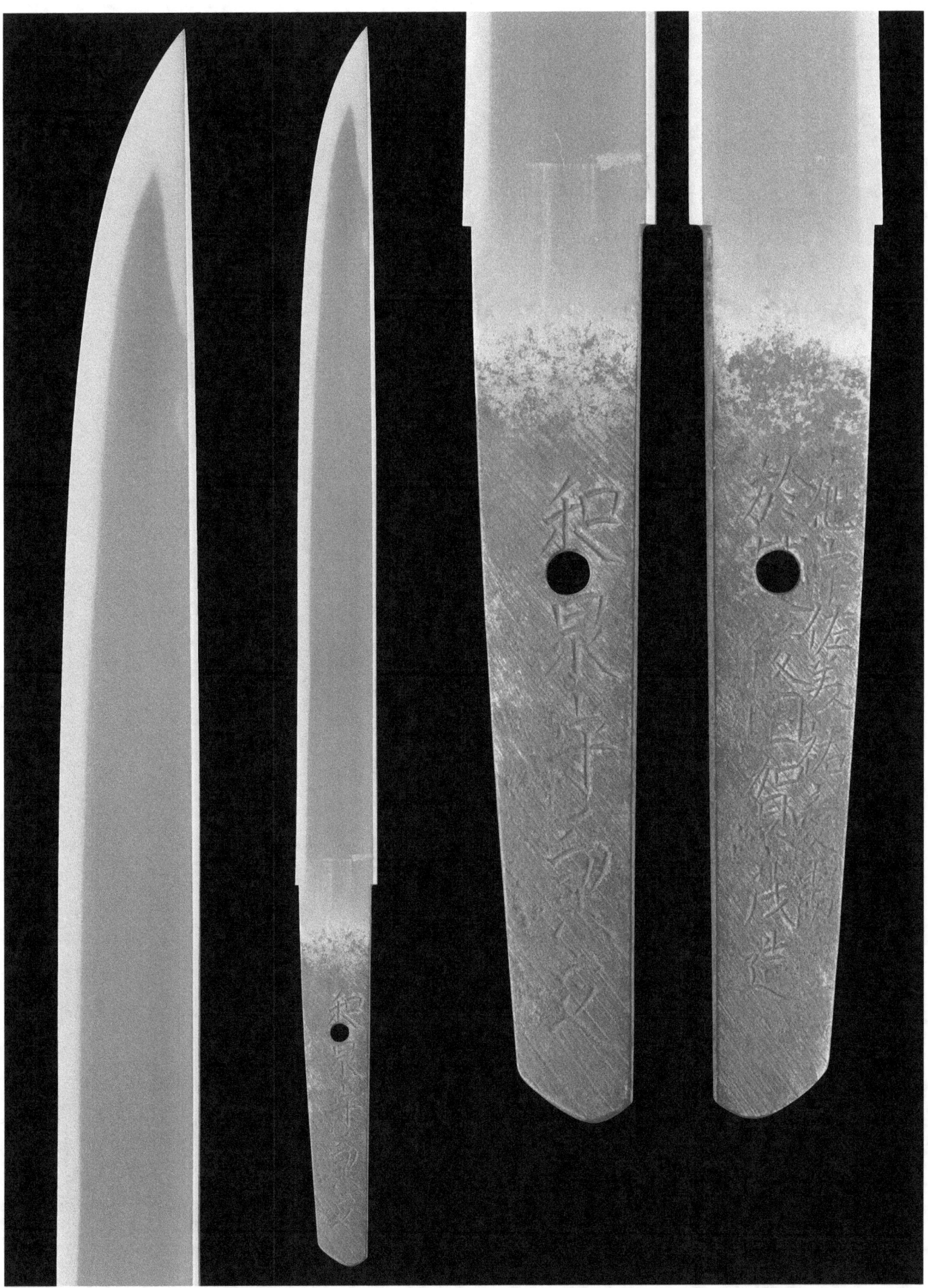

- 89 -

Tantō

Mei:
Omote: *Izumi no Kami Kanesada*
        和泉守兼定
Ura: *Echigo (no) kuni Kamo (ni) oite tsukuru*
        於越後国賀茂造
        Made at Kamo in Echigo province
Nagasa: 6 sun 7 bu 3 ri (20.4 cm)
Muzori

Jitetsu is very fine *Masame* with beautiful *Jinie*. *Hamon* is *ō-Notare* in deep *Nioi* as we find often this style in blades made in Kamo. When this *Tantō* was exhibited at Niigata History Museum the swordsmith Ōno Yoshimitsu who visited and he said that this *Sugata* was the best of Kanesada's *Tantō*.

(Toyama)

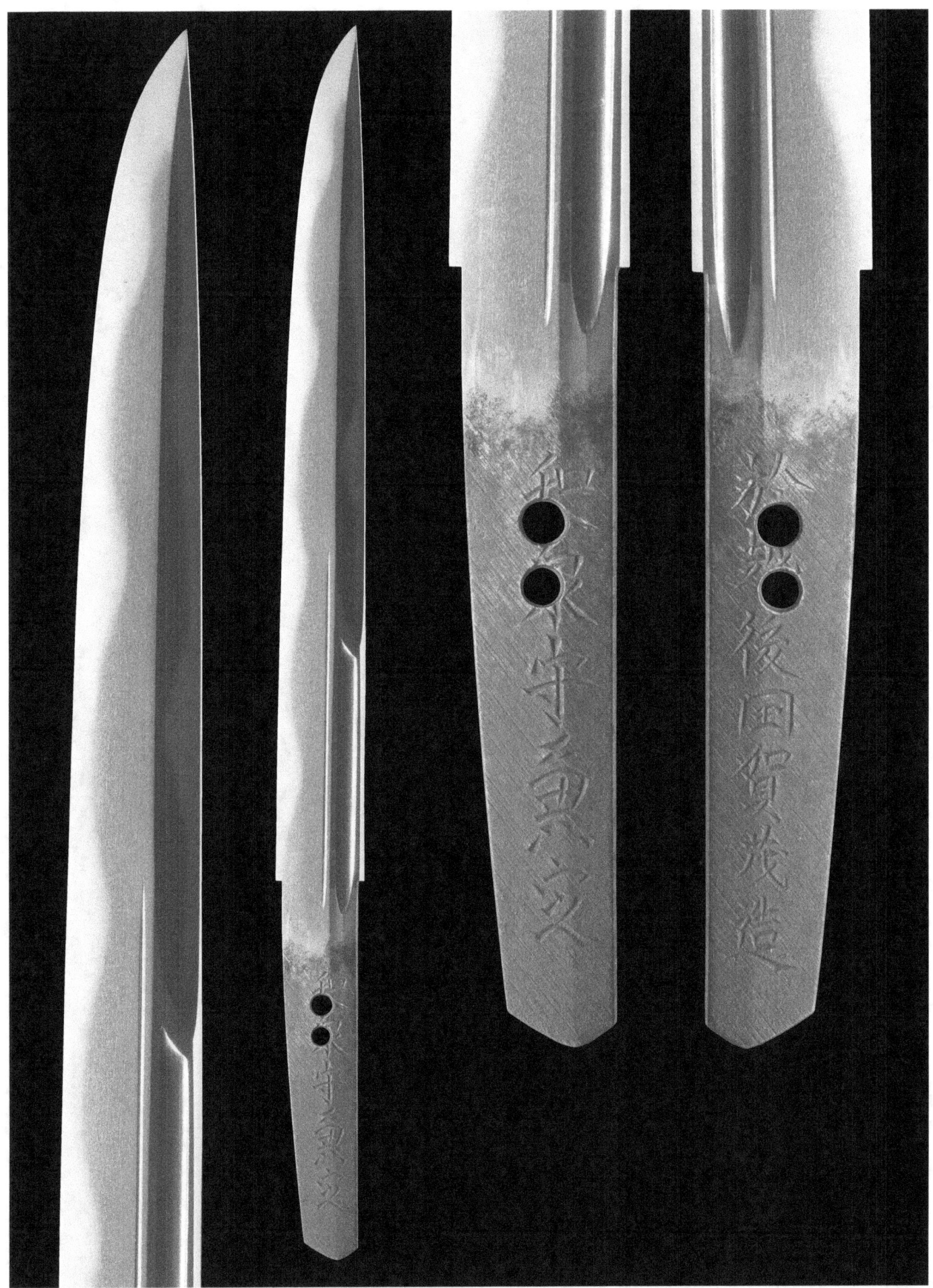

Wakizashi

Mei:
Omote: Iwashiro (no) kuni jū Izumi
        no Kami Kanesada
        岩代国住和泉守兼定
        Izumi no Kami Kanesada living
        in Iwashiro province
Ura: Echigo (no) kuni Kamo Seiren
        於越後国鴨渓精鍛
        Forged at Kamo in Echigo province
Nagasa: 1 shaku 8 sun (54.5 cm)
Sori: 3 bu (0.9 cm)

Wide *Mihaba* and not tapered, big stretched *Kissaki* makes magnificent *Sugata*. *Jitetsu* is *ō-Itamehada*. *Hamon* is *ō-Notare* in *Nioi-deki*. *Nioiguchi* of the lower parts of *Hamon* is very wide and deep, close to the cutting edge.

    Kanesada sometimes signed (鴨渓)"Kamo" as (加茂)"Kamo". This *Wakizashi* is an unusual workmanship which was made in Kamo.

(Toyama)

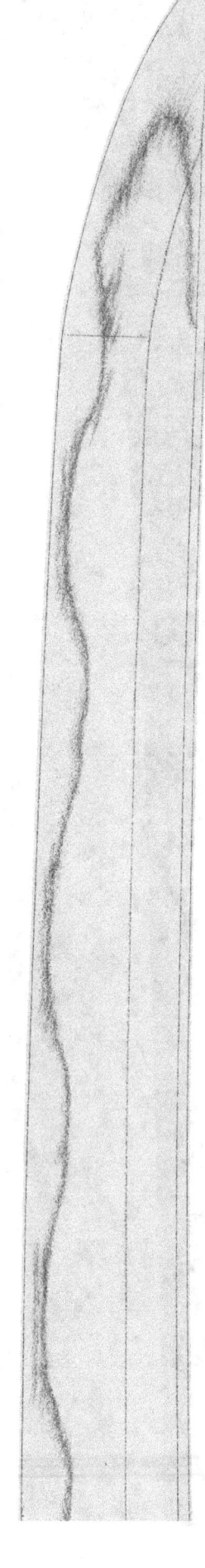

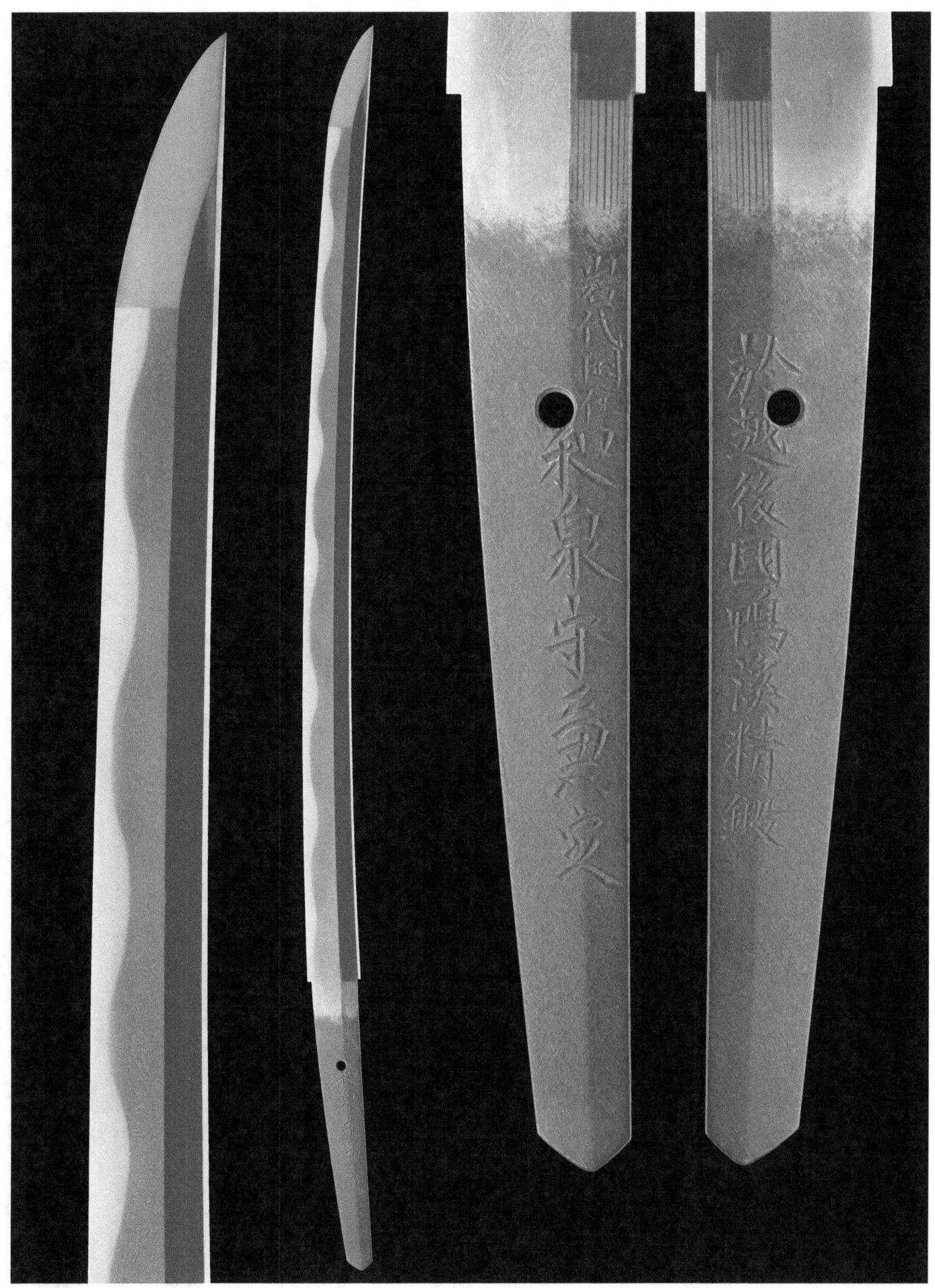

- 93 -

Tantō

Mei:
Omote: *Izumi no Kami Kanesada*
和泉守兼定
Ura: *Hokuetsu Kamo (ni) oite tsukuru*
於北越賀茂作
Made at Kamo in Hokuetsu
Nagasa: 7 sun 7 bu 6 ri (23.5 cm)
Muzori

Jitetsu is tight *ko-Mokume* mixed with *Itame*. *Hamon* is *ō-Gunome* tight *Nioiguchi*. *Mura-Nie* (spread *Nie*) in *Habuchi*, deep *Nie* in lower parts, a lot of activities in *Yakigashira*.

Bōshi turnback continue to *Gunome* became *Mune-yaki* till *Mune-machi*. The shape of this *Tantō* is from the particular period of late Muromachi era, it is so-called *Moroha-zukuri Tantō*. "Koshi no hiraita Gunome Hamon" reminding of *Sukesada* in Sue-Bizen style, very tight *Mokumehada*. It is showing high skills of Kanesada.

(Toyama)

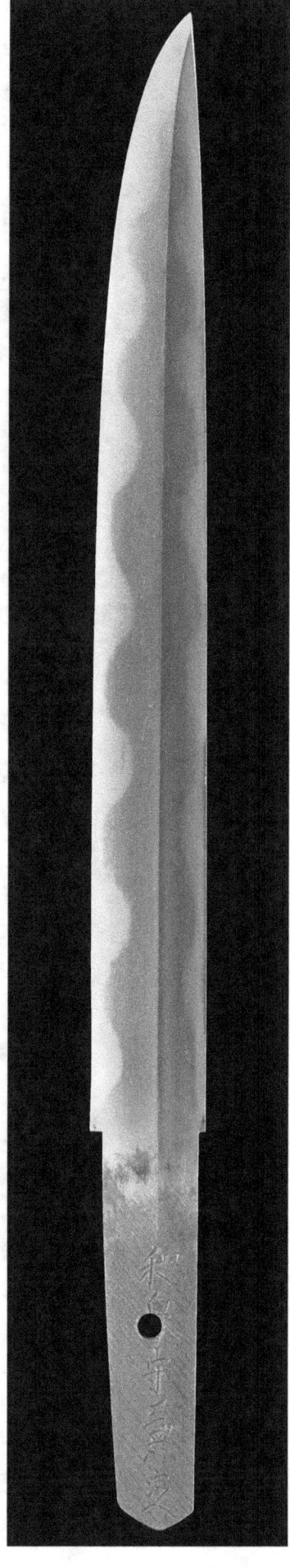

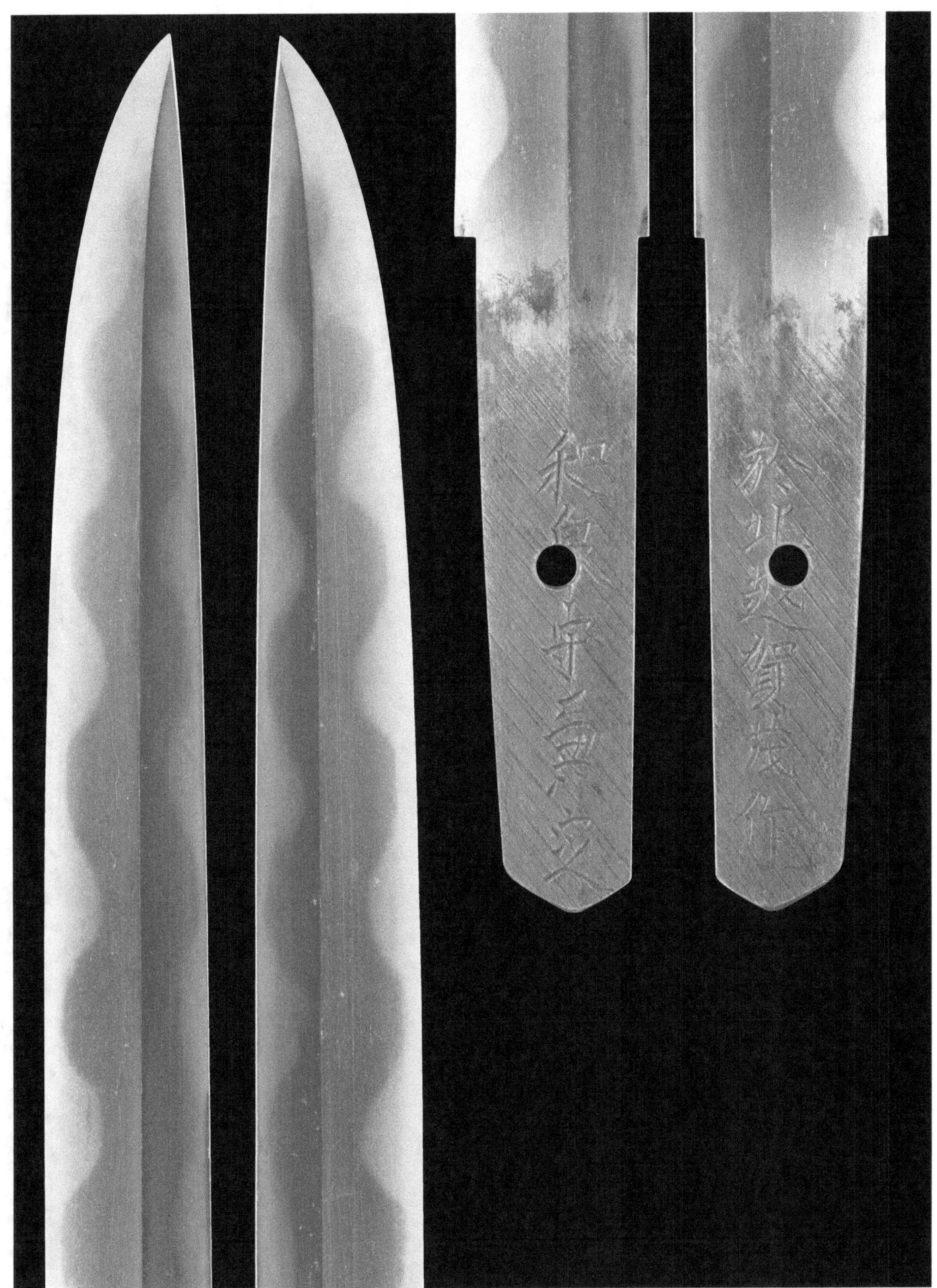

Tantō

Mei:
Omote: Izumi no Kami Kanesada
和泉守兼定
Ura: Shibata (ni) oite tsukuru
於新發田造
Made in Shibata
Nagasa: 4 sun 5 bu 5 ri (13.8 cm)
Uchizori

Sugata is *Hira-zukuri*, *Uchizori*. *Jitetsu* is tight *ko-Mokume*. *Hamon* is *ō-Notare*.

There is a *Katana* made by Kanesada donated to Suwa Jinja shrine in Shibata. We think that this *Tantō* was also made in Shibata at the same time. It is a very small *Tantō* however it has a very nice *Notare Hamon*.

(Toyama)

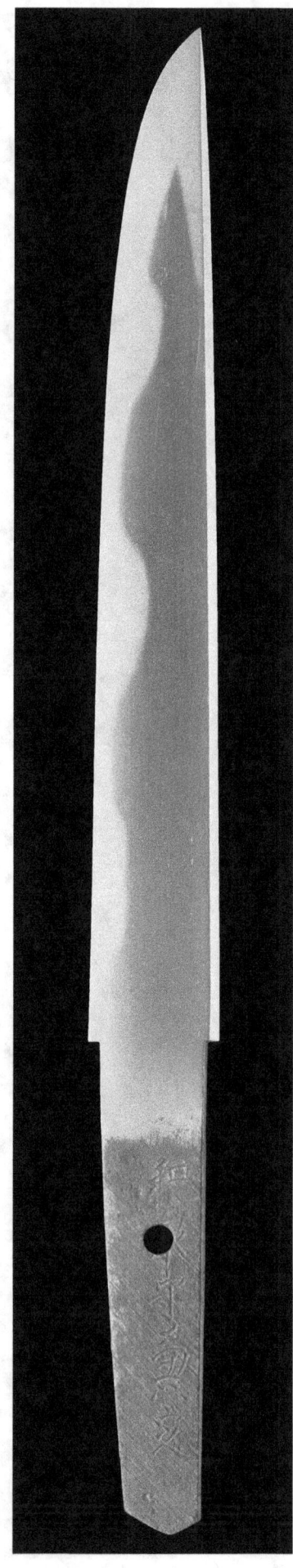

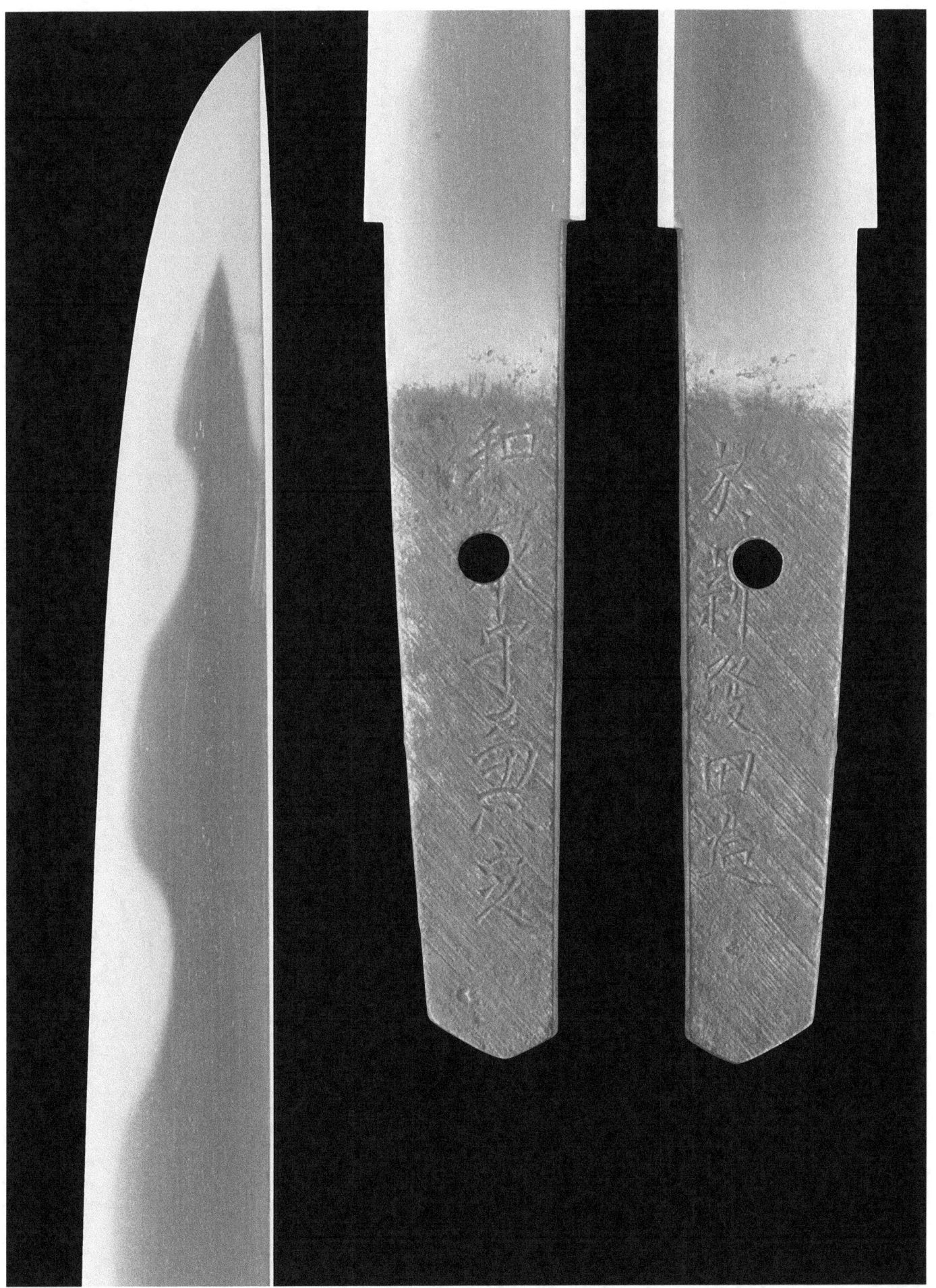

- 97 -

Tantō

Mei:
Omote: *Izumi no Kami Kanesada*
和泉守兼定
Ura: *Senshū-banzai*
千秋萬歳
A Thousand Years Long Life
Nagasa: *8 sun 5 ri* (18,3 cm)
Muzori

Here we have a blade in *Moroha-zukuri* what is rare for Kanesada. The *Jigane* is an *Itame* mixed with a hint of *Masame*. The *Hamon* on the *Mune* side is from the *Machi* to the tip a plain *Suguha*, and the one on the *Ha* side a pointed *Sanbonsugi Gunome*, tempered in a *Nie-deki*, whereat the *Nie* tend to *ko-Nie*. There is thick *Ashi* and *Sunagashi* in places and the *Deki* is excellent. The blade is undated but from the signature style we can place it somewhere around the time when Kanesada worked in Kamo. The slogan "Senshūbanzai" on the *Ura* side is found on blades from the Meiji era onwards. Before the Keiō era, he used the slogan "Kimibanzai."

(Kawashima)

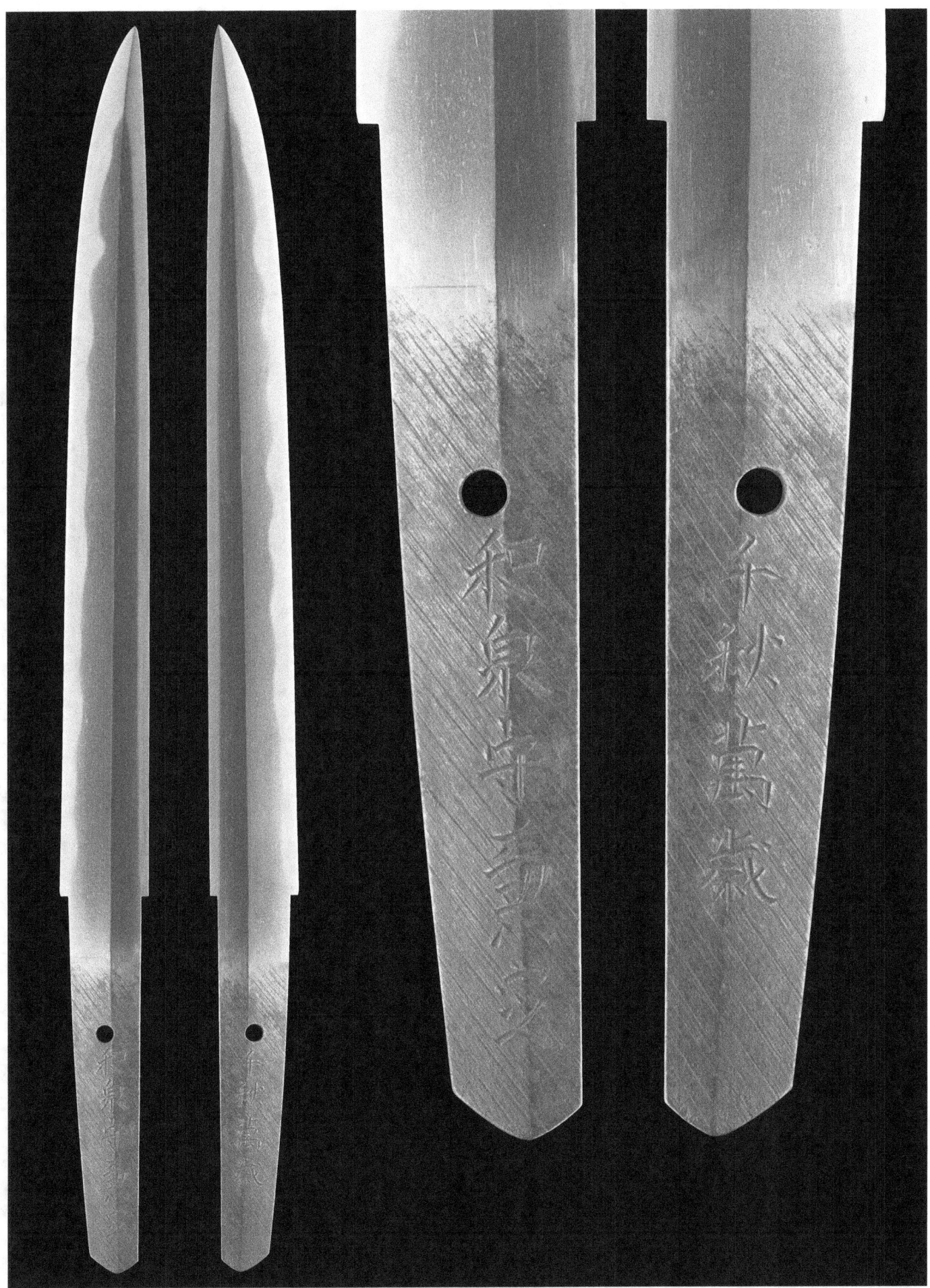

Tantō

Mei:
Omote: Kanesada
  兼定
Ura: *Senshū-banzai*
  千秋萬歳
  A Thousand Years Long Life
Nagasa: 8 sun 4 bu 5ri (25,6 cm)
Uchizori

The blade is in *Hira-zukuri* with a little *Uchizori* and has a relative scarce *Fukura* what is typical for the *Shinshintō* era. The *Sashi-omote* side shows *Gomabashi* and the *Sashi-ura* side a *Koshibi*. The *Jigane* is a very dense *ko-Itame* and the *Hamon* a *chū-Suguha* with some *Notare*, *Kuichigaiba* in places, and *Hotsure*. The *Nioiguchi* is quite tight and the *Nie* is uniformed.

On the basis of the signature style we can date this blade around the time when Kanesada worked in Kamo. It is likely that the change from the slogan "Kimibanzai" to "Senshū-banzai" goes back to the changes in time. "Kimibanzai" includes namely the character *Kimi* (君) which stands for the *Shōgun*. Before the Meiji Restoration and being a retainer of the Aizu fief, it suggests itself to sign with such a slogan but when times changed, the more neutral term "Senshū-banzai" became more appropriate. *Banzai* itself meens "Hurrah," "longlife," "congratulations" or "cheers". Literally it means "ten thousand years" and multiplies quasi the congratulary slogan "Senshū" which in turn means literally "thousand autumns."

(Kawashima)

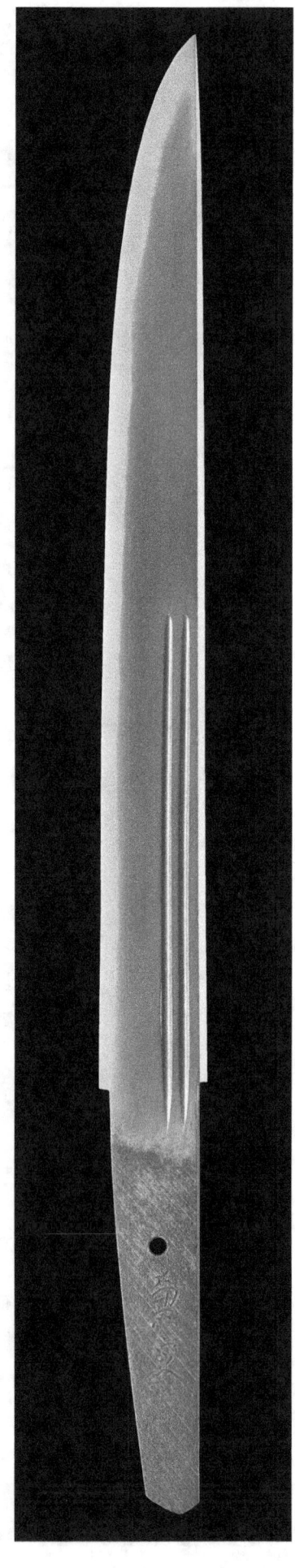

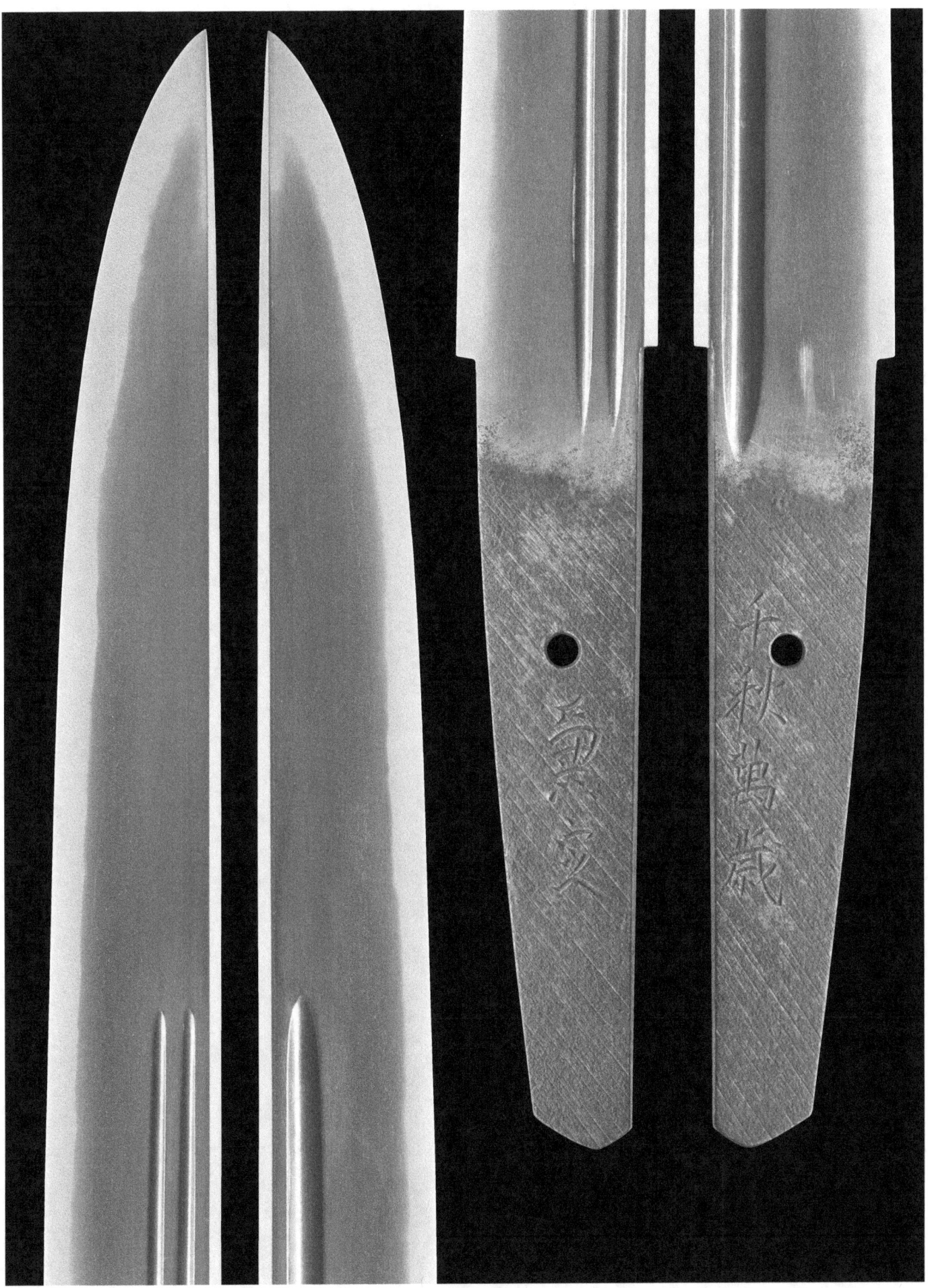

Katana

Mei:
Omote: *Dai Nihon – Kanesada*
大日本・兼定
Ura: *Kigen nisengohyakugojūninen nigatsu hi*
紀元二千五百五十二年二月日
A day of the second month of the 2,552nd anniversary of the imperial era
Nagasa: 2 shaku 2 sun 8 bu 4 ri (69,2 cm)
Sori: 5 *bu* (1,5 cm)

Kanesada was 55 years old in Meiji 25, i.e. the equivalent of the 2,552nd anniversary of the imperial era. This blade has a normal *Mihaba*, a high *Shinogi*, but a larger *Kissaki* than otherwise normally seen at Kanesada. The *Jigane* is a very dense *Masame* with *Chikei* and *Ji-nie* and the *Hamon* is ko-*Gunome* with *Togariba* in *Nie-deki* with plentiful of *Ashi* and some *Sunagashi* in places. That means the *Hamon* reminds of the Shizu school (志津) and is excellently done.

According to tradition, this is the blade Kanesada presented to the crown prince Yoshihito (嘉仁), the later emperor Taishō (大正天皇, 1879-1926). It is stored in a sword chest decorated with *Kikumon* (chrysanthemum crest) and *Kirimon* (paulownia crest). Yoneyama Ungai (米山雲外) wrote in his article "About the Aizu Swordsmith Izumi no Kami Kanesada" (Aizu-tōshō Izumi no Kami Kanesada ni tsuite, 会津刀匠和泉守兼定について), published in the issue 55 of the Tōken-Bijutsu, that the smith presented on the fourth day of the sixth month Meiji 25 a *Katana* to the crown prince. The present was favorably received and he was rewarded with a 10 Yen gold coin. But Kanesada made two *Katana* at that time. The other one, also has *ō-Kissaki*, which is rare for him. It was offered by Koteda Yasusada (籠手田安定, 1840-1899), the then governor of Niigata Prefecture, to the Iyahiko-jinja (弥彦神社). This shrine held the highest shrine rank (Ichinomiya, 一宮) of Echigo province which had become Niigata Prefecture.

(Kawashima)

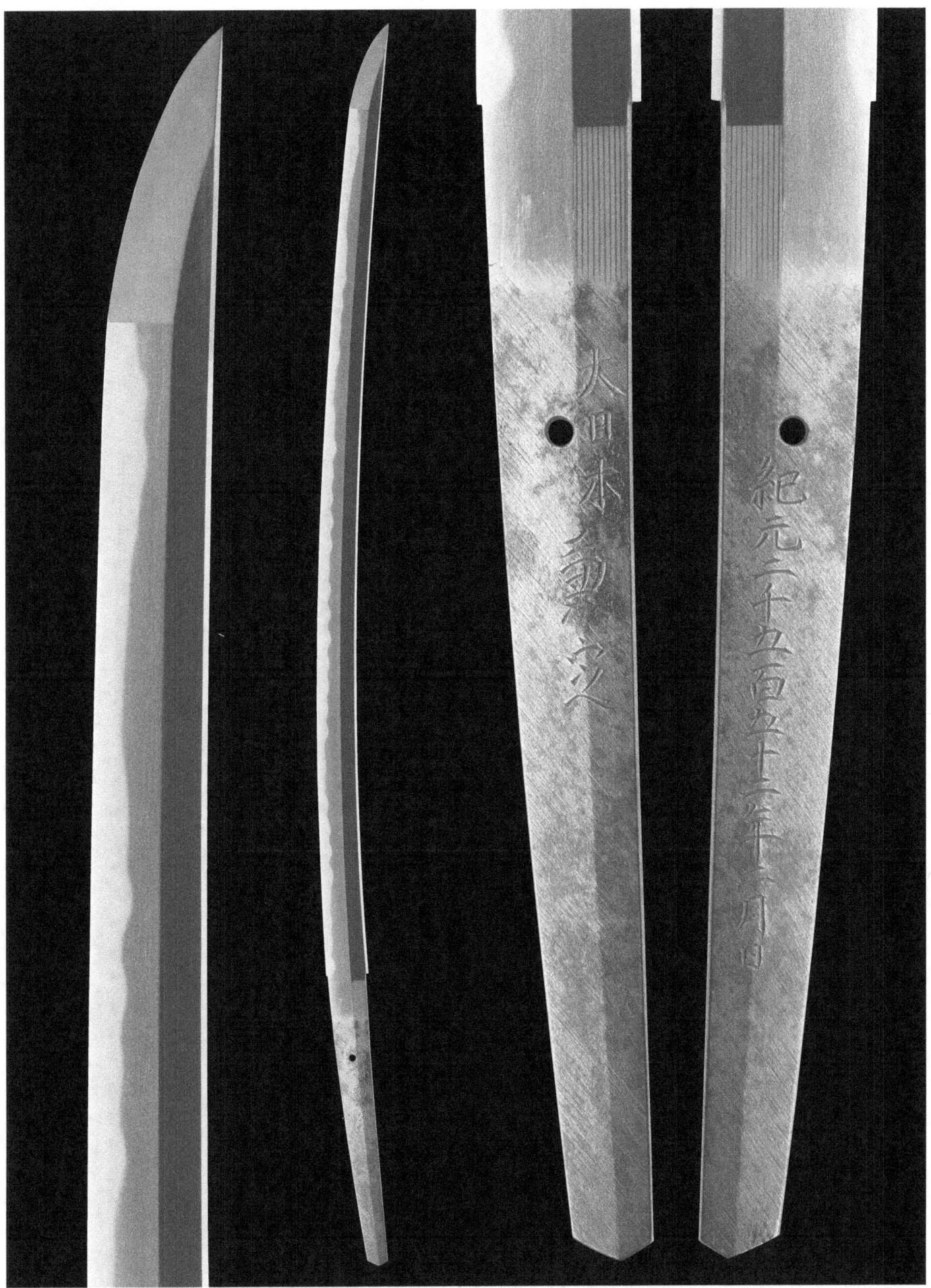

- 103 -

Katana

Mei:
Omote: *Izumi no Kami Kanesada*
和泉守兼定
Ura: *Meiji nijūhachinen sangatsu jūkunichi*
明治二十八年三月十九日
19th day of the third month Meiji 28 [1895]
Nagasa: *2 shaku 1 sun 7 bu 8 ri* (66,0 cm)
Sori: *3 bu 6 ri* (1,1 cm)

Kanesada was 59 years old when he made that blade. The *Sugata* has normal proportions and dimensions but shows a high *Shinogi*. The *Kitae* is an *Itame* mixed with *Mokume* and *Chikei* and *Ji-nie* appear. The *Hamon* is a *Sanbonsugi*-like *Gunome* with uniform *Yakigashira*. Plentiful of *ko-Nie* accumulate in the valleys of the *Gunome* and there are also many *Ashi*. The *Bōshi* is widely tempered and appears as *Jizō*-like *Midare-komi*. A blade with an excellent *Deki* which displays the fully matured workmanship of the older Kanesada.

(Kawashima)

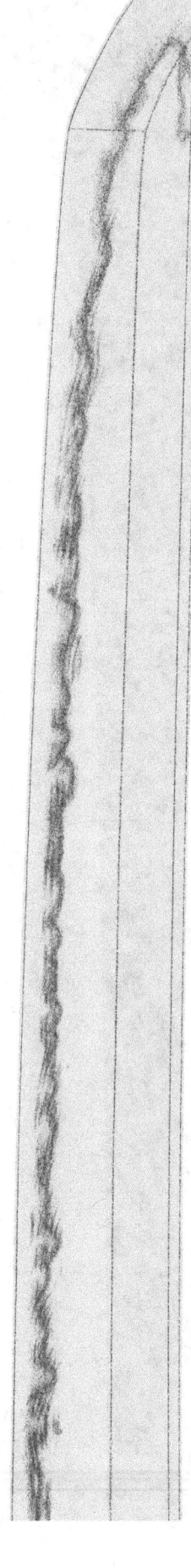

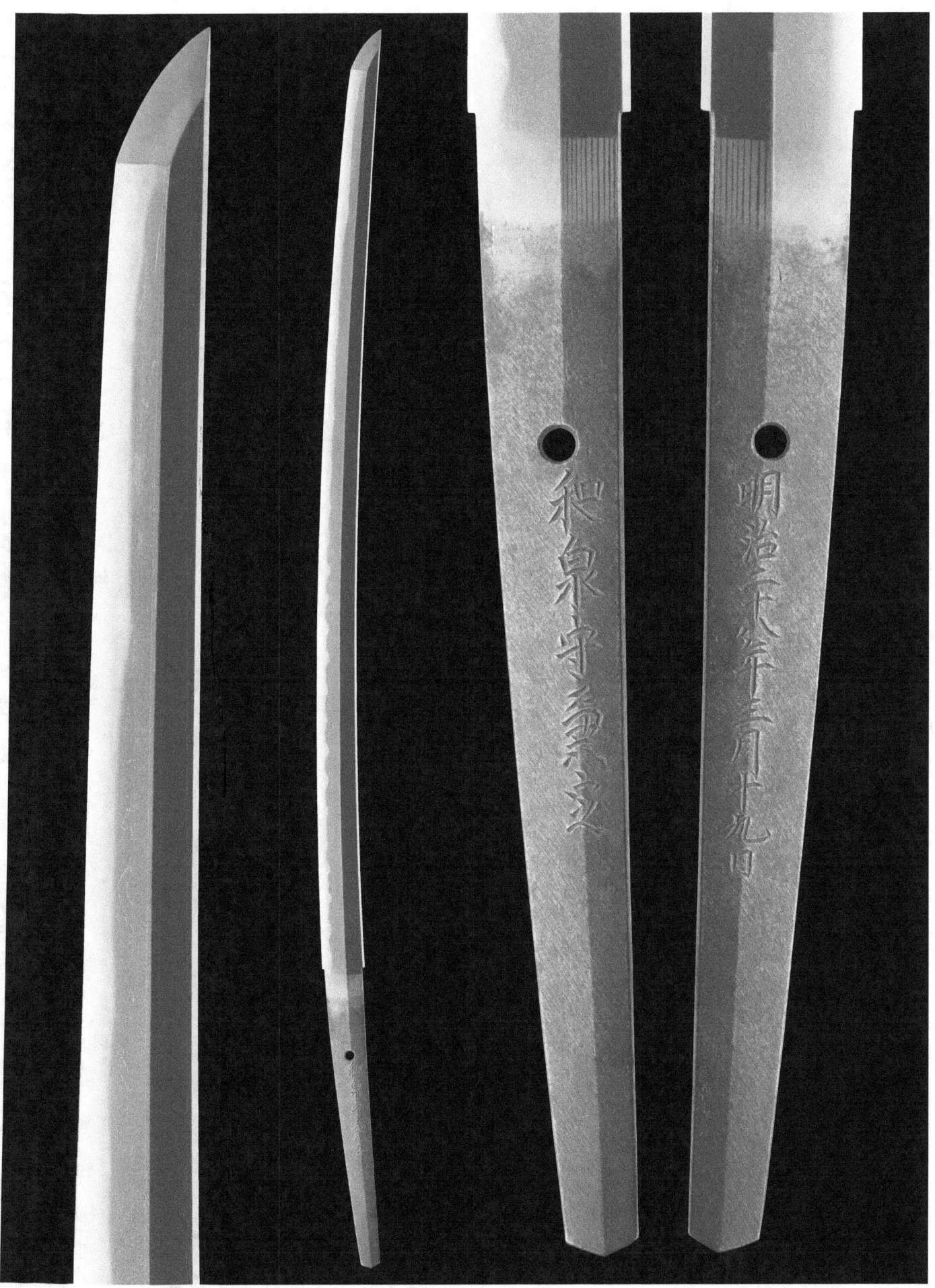

和泉守藤原兼定
明治丁丑年十二月十九日

Tantō

Mei:
Omote: *Kanesada*
兼定
Ura: *Meiji sanjūgonen ichigatsu futsuka*
明治三十五年一月二日
Second day of the first month
Meiji 35 [1902]
Nagasa: 5 *sun* 8 *ri* (15,4 cm)
Muzori

Kanesada was 65 years old in Meiji 35 (1902). He died the very next year so this *Tantō* is one of his latest works. It is in *Hira-zukuri* and rather short, even for a *Tantō*, but has compared to the *Nagasa* a relatively thick *Kasane*. The *Kitae* is a very dense *ko-Itame* with *Ji-nie*. The *Hamon* is a wide *Gunome* and the *Bōshi* a widely tempered *Jizō*-like *Notare-komi*. The tempering is in *Nie-deki* and the *Nioiguchi* is wide and even we are facing as mentioned "just" a small *Tantō*, it is nevertheless full of vigor.

The *Shirasaya* of this *Tantō* bears a *Sayagaki* written by Kanesada himself. It reads: "Meiji sanjūgonen ichigatsu kitae, musume no Yoshiko e sakusha no okurutokoro – toki ni rokujūgo-sai" (明治三十五年一月鍛娘よしこへ作者の贈るところ・ときに六十五歳, "forged in the first month of Meiji 35 and at the age of 65 as a present for my daughter Yoshiko"), and makes the *Tantō* a very precious reference piece.

(Kawashima)

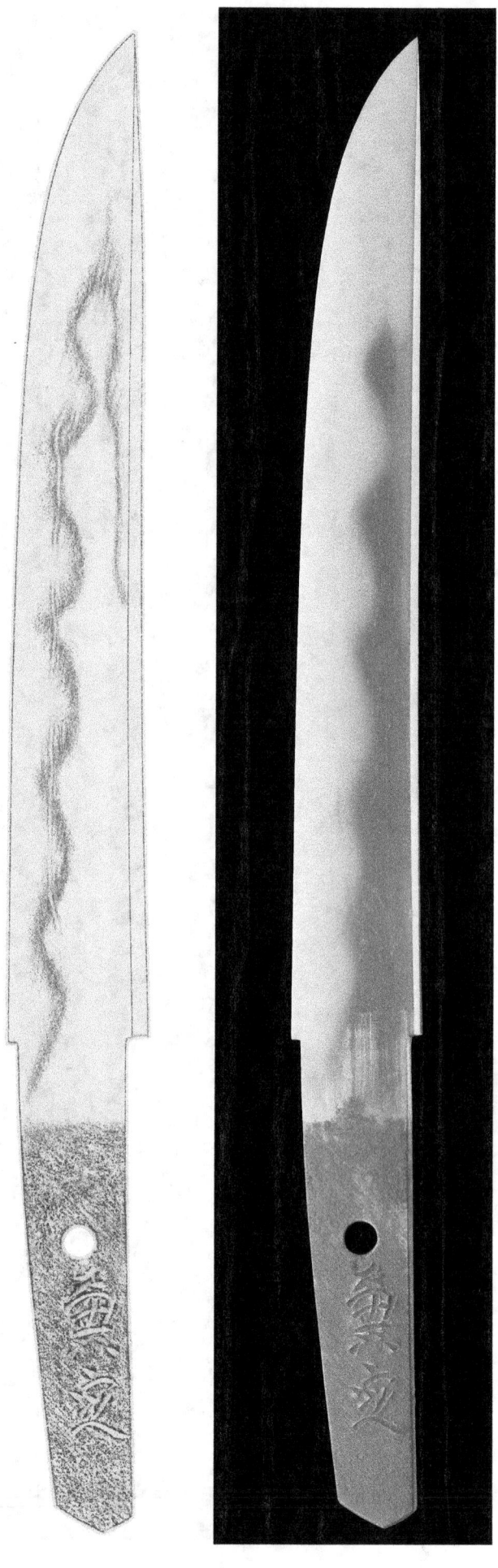

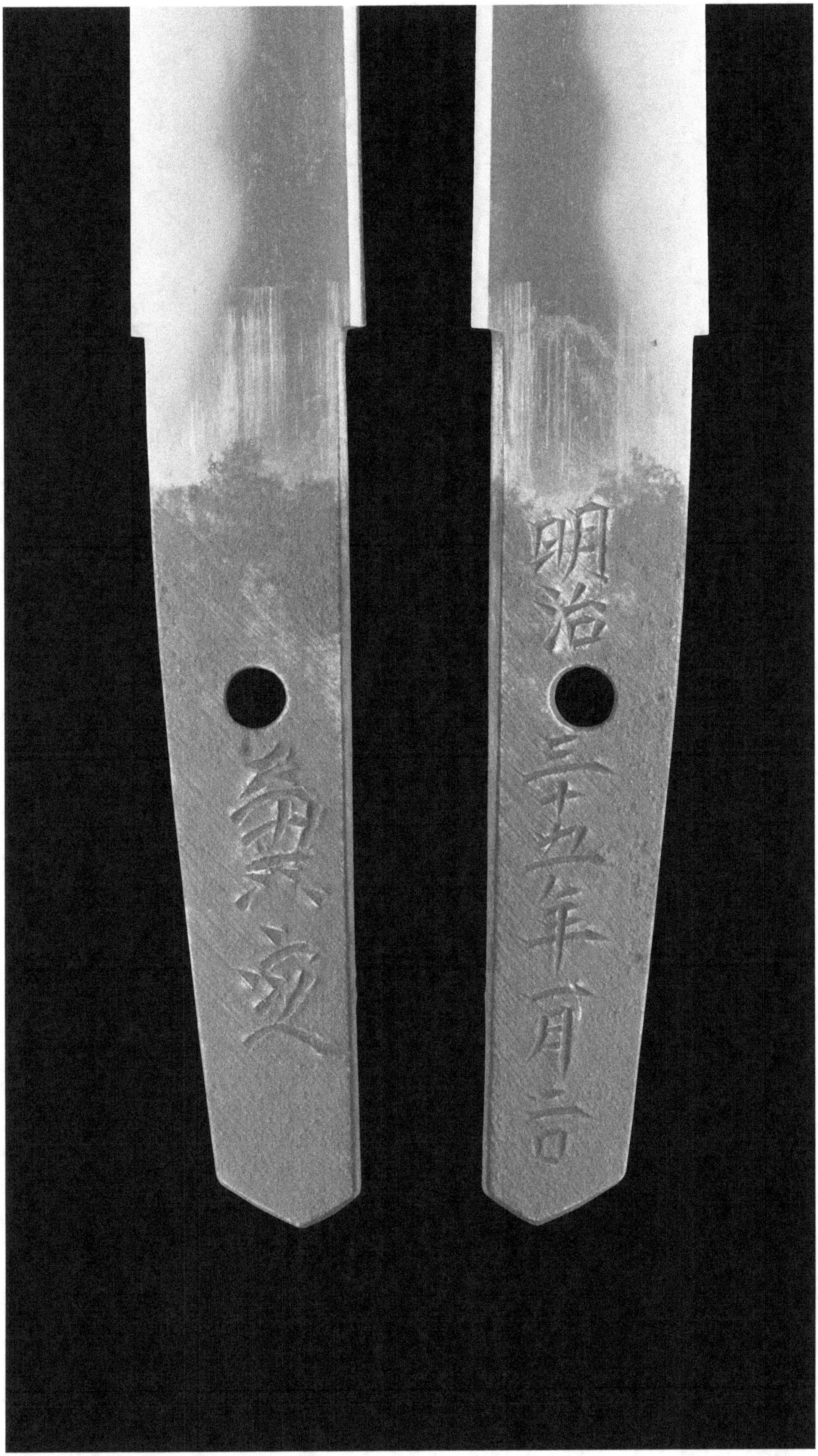

表：栗原信秀

裏：明治卅五年八月日

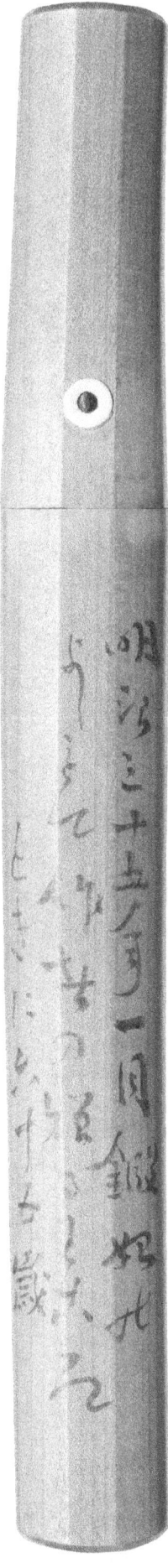

明治三十五年一同鍛如此
よって外其の證となし、
ともに永持す可し

www.ingramcontent.com/pod-product-compliance
Lightning Source LLC
Chambersburg PA
CBHW081118240526
45470CB00019B/2610